The Holocaust in Hebrew Literature
From Genocide To Rebirth

Alan J. Yuter

National University Publications
ASSOCIATED FACULTY PRESS
Port Washington, N.Y. // 1983

National University Publications
ASSOCIATED FACULTY PRESS

Series in Judaic Studies

Advisory Editor
Honorable Seymour R. Levine

Manufactured in the United States of America

Published by
Associated Faculty Press, Inc.
Port Washington, N.Y.

Library of Congress Cataloging in Publication Data

Yuter, Alan J., 1946–
    The Holocaust in Hebrew literature, from genocide to rebirth.

    (National university publications)
    Bibliography: p.
    1. Israeli literature—History and criticism.
2. Holocaust, Jewish (1939-1945), in literature.
3. Holocaust survivors in literature. I. Title.
PJ5012.H65Y87   1983   892.4'6'09358   83-9973
ISBN 0-8046-5322-4

TO EVA AND MISHA,

for whom the Holocaust was not the end

Contents

i

Acknowledgements

This study of the Hebrew literature of the Holocaust in English translation would not have been possible without the support, attention, encouragement and sound professional advice of many.

My thanks go to Professor Byron Sherwin of the Spertus College of Judaica, under whose auspices this study was conceived, and to the Hyman and Susan Wein Foundation of Chicago, Illinois, whose generous grant enabled me to collect materials and allocate the time necessary for thoughtful research.

For my teachers, professors and colleagues who have guided and encouraged my research, I am especially grateful. Professor Samuel Leiter of the Jewish Theological Seminary of America was my first serious instructor in the craft of literary analysis, and Professor Dan Miron of the Hebrew University impressed upon me the importance of value, aesthetic taste, and historical context in literary scholarship. Professors Baruch A. Levine, Milton Arfa, and M.L. Rosenthal of New York University provided me with the critical tools of mature literary analysis.

Drs. Menahem Schmelzer, and Herman Dicker of the library of the Jewish Theological Seminary of America, and Dr. Berry Gittlen, of the Baltimore Hebrew College, placed their time and resources at my disposal, and enabled me to find the necessary sources for my research. I thank them for their patience, understanding and thoughtfulness.

I must also thank my wife, Linda, for the hours I did not share with her, and my children, Esther and Joshua, for their putting up with a scholarly absentee father.

Foreword

Despite the cynicism and doubt that one expects to find in works of Holocaust fiction and poetry, one striking motif recurs throughout the Hebrew literary response to modern Jewry's most terrible tragedy. The classical Jewish doctrinal question of salvation is omnipresent in the narratives, themes, and symbols of the two generations of writers and poets who have reacted, sensitively and artistically, to the trauma of the years 1939-1945.[1]

Although different writers have differing views concerning the nature and possibility of redemption, these concerns are common to most. This observation is based on the research conducted for the present study and is not grounded in any political or theological bias.[2]

Because this volume is intended for the English-speaking reader who is interested in Israeli Holocaust literature, the number of works available for discussion is limited. Further translations of Israeli Holocaust literature will, no doubt, require a more exhaustive treatment.

Alan J. Yuter

Chapter 1

The Holocaust Victim and Survivor in Fiction

Ka-Tzetnik

When *Atrocity,* which is a powerful novel by Ka-Tzetnik[3] portraying the sexual abuse of a principled little Jewish boy in the concentration camp at Auschwitz was published in Israel, it was well received by the rightist press. The reviewer for the Orthodox Zionist organ, *Ha-Tzofe* wrote:

> The author regards himself as the keeper of a chronicle. Indeed, the essential importance of the book is its documentary side second to which is its literary rendering. It is the very documentation which I see as a major literary achievement.[4]

The reviewer in the religiously oriented weekly *Panim el Panim* emphasized Ka-Tzetnik's presentation of European Jewry's suffering at the hands of the Nazis, and concluded that this "book of revelation is a holy book." *Ha-Boker*, a right-of-center Zionist publication, was concerned with the work's "historical timeliness" and the dehumanization of the "Jewish block orderlies who forfeited their membership in the human race."[5] The jingoistic nationalism of secular as well as religious reviews underscores the suffering of European Jewry; the enthusiasm for the novel was largely based on what the reviewers perceived to be an endorsement of their ideological position. When Ka-Tzetnik's next novel, *Phoenix Over the Galilee*, which calls for reconciliation and rapprochement with the Palestinian Arabs as a remedy for the hatred spawned by the Holocaust was published, it was hailed by *Al Youm*, Israel's Arabic daily newspaper; by *Hatha al-Aalam*, an Israeli-Arabic weekly; and by Professor Bar Hillel, a philosophy professor at the Hebrew University with leftist leanings.[6] While these different ideologues found in Ka-Tzetnik's work a reflection of their own views, they did so at the expense of a critical reading of the fiction they were analyzing. The present examination of Ka-Tzetnik's writing must of necessity focus upon the world view that underlies his fiction. Since *Phoenix Over the Galilee* and *Atrocity* reflect the views of a single author, it is incumbent upon the literary critic and exegete to define this underlying outlook as a prolegomenon to a more objective definition of this writer's response to the Holocaust.

Ka-Tzetnik's three novels—*Atrocity, House of Dolls,* and *Phoenix Over the Galilee* trace the fates of three siblings—Moni, Daniella, and Harry Preleshnik— during the Holocaust, and in the case of Harry, afterward.[7] In *Atrocity*, Moni, a gentle seven-year-old boy is taken from his parents and placed in the concentration camp where he becomes a homosexual prostitute in order to survive.

In *House of Dolls*—which was the first novel in the series to be published—Daniella is inducted into what is euphemistically referred to as "House of Dolls," a barracks where sterilized prostitutes who must "entertain" German soldiers returning from the front. Moni and Daniella both die, but the fact that they physically succumb testifies only to the limits of their physical endurance, for they sustain their moral integrity until the end. Neither of them ever forget the traditional loyalty and love that they had experienced in their home before they were thrust into the hell of Auschwitz.

Harry alone—the oldest of the three—survives physically, but he emerges mentally broken and spiritually crippled, lacking both the will to live and the ability to love. What he lost by survival, his younger sister and brother preserved through death. Once liberated from Auschwitz, Harry has somehow to rediscover his moral and human bearings. It is through Galilea Glick, a young Israeli, that Harry learns to love and to reenter human society, but in nursing Harry to spiritual health, Galilea herself becomes overwhelmed by the terrible hatreds and fears that plagued Harry. Together they finally heal each other through their love, and by transforming their vengeful hatred for the Germans and their obsession with death and the past into understanding sympathy for the Israeli Arabs. Ka-Tzetnik does not suggest that naive faith in a redeeming love will bring about the world's salvation. He offers the reader instead a disquieting challenge, for he does believe that it is only love of one's fellow that makes moral redemption possible. Humanity's salvation nonetheless remains in doubt.

Harry reaches Israel a psychological cripple; he must reconcile himself somehow with the dreadful past and regain his identity.[7]

Unlike Harry, however, neither Moni in *Atrocity* nor Daniella in *House of Dolls* ever really grasp the enormity of their situation. Their innocent naiveté, which serves to protect their integrity, inhibits their response to a world so grotesque and evil that it is beyond their comprehension. All three of Ka-Tzetnik's novels begin in *media res*, from a point after the earliest action in the novels. As in Greek tragedy, Ka-Tzetnik has created an epic tragedy in a modern setting.[8] In the cases of Moni and Daniella, their tragic flaw is their humanity and naive integrity. Their deaths are the result of their inability to perceive, and, as a consequence, to adapt themselves to the horror and dehumanization to which they are subjected.[9]

House of Dolls, the first of Ka-Tzetnik's three-part chronicle, presents three contrasting themes: the dehumanizing setting of Auschwitz; Harry's will to live and struggle to maintain his humanity in an environment that constantly calls for his abdication of moral responsibility; and Daniella's initiation into a demonic adulthood for which she, by dint of her refinement and values, is unprepared to face. In spite of the moral outrages Ka-Tzetnik describes, he never interjects his own subjective personal observations or value judgments. The novel's meaning surfaces through the ironic and tragic juxtaposition of human values as they are reflected in the persons of Daniella and Harry and the totally evil, sadistic forces that operate upon them in Auschwitz.

Nazi genocide is not the only source of dehumanization in *House of Dolls*. The Polish partisans who escaped the Nazi invasion, presently turn to shooting those Jews who have managed to survive also forfeit their humanity. They are the same Poles who, in the name of patriotism, accuse the Jews of betraying the mother land and with the Nazi conquest, "turned overnight into *Volksdeutsche*" German nationals, whose allegiance is to the German nation even though they do not live within its territory.

The Polish Jews themselves are not immune to the pressures that compromise their humanity. The members of the Judenrat, the autonomous Jewish council, give preference to the richer Jews under their jurisdiction at the expense of the poorer ones in their selection of who is to live and who is to die. Monyek Montroz, the head of the Judenrat, uses his position to assign Fella, a beautiful young Jewish girl whom he finds troublesome, to the House of Dolls, realizing all the while that in so doing he is consigning her to a life of prostitution, if not death. When soup is distributed, the starving trample upon each other for the few bowls allocated. Significantly, the Judenrat selects those who have availed themselves of the soup when the Gestapo demands the quota of Jews to be sentenced to death. Even those starved Jews who stand in line for soup know that they do so at their lives' peril. One cannot read Ka-Tzetnik's *House of Dolls* as a polemic against Nazi inhumanity alone; it is a critique, orchestrated with sordidly grotesque detail, of man's inhumanity to his fellow human beings.

The primary crime perpetrated in Auschwitz against humanity is the arbitrary and torturous murder of another person. A more subtle assault upon human dignity that takes place at Auschwitz is the creation of the Mussulmen, human skeletons seemingly held together by their bones alone, in whom the will to live no longer throbs. The "eyes of Mussulmen stare blankly," like the living corpses which they are. Those women who were worked to death eventually become "Mussulmanesses that crawl of their own accord into the van, appearing like a death crawl of corpses returning voluntarily from the night, one after the other, into their common burial pit." A Mussulman is a nonperson who is spiritually dead and physically numb; he moves with complete inertia until he is mercifully released by death:

> Everything is mirrored in the eyes, from the first hint of Mussulmanishness to the oncoming end. THE EYES. . . . The well-known Mussulman eyes. . . .First they mirror the calcifying soul, only then the calcified body.

When speaking about the corpses of these Mussulmen, the concentration camp medical orderlies among whom Harry works refer to them as "shit." In a desperate struggle to maintain his humanity and dignity, Harry fights the feeling that he, too, is becoming a Mussulman; he begins to fear that his struggle is in vain when he notices that his hands are calcified and gnarled and that his time is largely spent among corpses and with Mussulmen.

Those assigned to the work details at Auschwitz die a slow death, while their strength and will to live are drained away by degrading, backbreaking labor. Those like Daniella who are condemned to the House of Dolls are sexually violated and, when they suffer three "reports" that they have failed to satisfy the appetites of the German soldiers, they are condemned to die by public bludgeoning. Ka-Tzetnik's use of sacred symbolism in the *House of Dolls* infuses the demonic setting with an ironic quality. The "reports" that the Jewish "dolls" receive for "having failed to appreciate the honor of satisfying a German warrior" are called sins.

The remedy or penance for them is termed "purgation," or purification by death. Two members of the House of Dolls—the pious *Bet Ya'akov* girls, Hannah and Tzivia, maintain their innocence and chastity until their deaths. Unwilling to have her body defiled, Tzivia cheerfully accepts her three "reports" for refusing the advances of the German soldiers to whom she is assigned, all the while realizing that her refusal will result in her "purgation."

The ultimate defilement of Daniella's dignity occurs after she is assigned to the House of Dolls. Living there, she is neither starved nor physically overworked to the point of exhaustion. Unlike the girls and women in the work force, Daniella and the other members of the House of Dolls are well fed and live comfortably until such a time as they have received their three deadly reports. The women on the work force begrudge the conscripted prostitutes the sausage, the bread and margarine, and the two cups of soup that they feel rightfully belongs to them. Ka-Tzetnik thus contrasts the indignities suffered by the inmates of the House of Dolls and the short-sightedness of those on the labor detail.

While the Auschwitz setting—frequently referred to in the book as "another planet,"—is one of terror and horror, Daniella preserves her moral integrity by refusing to renounce her family standards. Separated from her family by the Nazis at the outbreak of war when she is off on a school excursion, she is taken to Auschwitz and inducted into the House of Dolls and is sterilized, but she never surrenders her personal integrity. While she knows that she must eat if she is to satisfy the German soldiers, Daniella is unable to do so. Her moral sensitivity is also reflected in her inability to tell Tzevia of her sister's death lest she upset her unnecessarily. Once Daniella enters Auschwitz, the photographs of her family and childhood, the sources of her values, are taken from her and destroyed because they are "shit." Nevertheless, her naiveté and her upbringing shield her from her hellish environment. Unlike the Mussulmen, for whom love, loyalty, and human devotion no longer exist, Daniella survives for a while by daydreaming of a better past, which helps to reinforce her innate moral values. When finally her resistance falters, she makes the bid for freedom that ends in her death. By including in his account of Daniella's death the sentry's pleasure at earning a pass by aiming his rifle correctly and killing her, Ka-Tzetnik underscores the moral callousness of the individual sentry in particular and of the Auschwitz community in general. Daniella's character is never impunged, not even in death.

Daniella's brother, Harry, is saved from becoming a Mussulman in Auschwitz because he is assigned to serve as a medic; his white uniform partly anesthetizes him to the horrors of loading for burial the mounds of Jewish corpses, which as a medic, he is required to oversee. Like Daniella—and, for that matter, like Moni in *Atrocity*— Harry cannot eat even though there is sufficient food available to him. Eating would be a further profanation of the lives extinguished by starvation. While he cannot bring himself to eat, Harry nonetheless does struggle to keep himself from becoming a Mussulman. Like the Mussulmen he does not eat; unlike the Mussulman, his own integrity and will to live do not allow him to deny his values by capitulating to his hideous dehumanized environment. When he is no longer able to shed a tear for what he feels is his ebbing humanity, he fears that he, too, may well become a Mussulman.

In *House of Dolls*, through the use of interior monologue and flashback, Daniella's struggle to survive spiritually in a world of hell and insanity is made vividly clear:

> Two existences. Severed and sundered. No connection or bridge between them. Which is reality and which is nightmare?. . .Can she be living these two separate lives simultaneously?

Her only means of escape is death, for the dead alone are free of what those who are alive in Auschwitz must endure. By seeking to escape and meeting her death, Daniella does indeed escape Auschwitz. Her death also embodies the one less that she has to bequeath to her friend, the more sophisticated Fella:

> At that moment, all feeling of hatred seemed to evaporate from her [Fella]. At that moment her hatred toward the Germans swept over all the bounds of her senses. So deep was this hate, she could no longer see it. . . .
> She couldn't get herself to hate the Judenrat—they were so puny, so no-account as against the tidal waves of misery breaking around her. . . .She couldn't even hate God, now.

The despair that Fella reaches when she realizes the fact of Daniella's death is an anticipation of what Harry eventually experiences in *Phoenix Over the Galillee*. In Auschwitz, all die either physically or spiritually.

The second of Ka-Tzetnik's novels to be published, *Atrocity*, is, like *House of Dolls*, a *Bildungsroman*, which describes the introduction and the subsequent testing of Moni in Auschwitz. As in

House of Dolls, Ka-Tzetnik vividly describes the sexual exploitation of Jewish children, the plight of the Mussulmen, and the moral depravity of those who supervise the inevitable deaths and burials of the inmates of the concentration camp. The novel's principal focus is upon the first initiation of a gentle seven-year-old boy—a child who might otherwise have grown up to be a cultivated, sensitive adult—into a crazed absurd world that will either subject him to homosexual advances by older men or have him slowly and painfully starve to death. Like Daniella, Moni's heroism is embodied in his innocent integrity and will to live.

He is first described in *House of Dolls* as a small child who has inherited his mother's soft, velvety eyes and her air of rabbinic aristocracy. These inherited characteristics make him an attractive *Piepel*—a child homosexual prostitute. His first block chief, Franzel, calls him a doll; he tells Moni that his eyes have appeal, and that he is truly a prize. The values of the culture Moni represents are antithetical to the role he now assumes in order to survive. Nevertheless, he learns to bear the tension created by his will to live, his inability to accommodate himself to homosexual prostitution, and the threat of succumbing to a Mussulman death in life, which awaits him if he does not accept the perverted conventions of concentration camp life.

In Moni's Auschwitz, human dignity no longer exists for either the torturers or the tortured. One Nazi official after lovemaking, invariably chokes his victim to death. Another minor Nazi official is known as Holy Dad, being so designated because he has a remarkably auspicious ability to devise for his victims unusually painful deaths. Another—Fruchenbaum—who once was a *Piepel* himself, chops one of Moni's fellows to death for reminding him of the Jewish roots he has earlier denied in accepting Auschwitz's demonic order. Even the Polish watchmen are too bored to concern themselves with those inmates who are beaten because "its all shit." Once one's expression of concern for one's fellow is reduced to the level of excrement, the quality of human life has become debased and circumscribed beyond moral recognition. Exposure to inhuman suffering desensitizes even those who experience such suffering relatively little. The imprisoned Poles even resent the position of the Jews in the potato peeleries— since the Jews alone are fodder for the crematoria, their places could better be served by giving it to a Pole who, unlike a Jew, would almost certainly survive the war.

As in *House of Dolls*, the Mussulmen are the most benumbed of the Auschwitz victims. It is they who are chosen to guard the rations because in them "the nasty urge to eat has atrophied." "Mussulmen

are neither asleep nor awake: they neither lie nor sit." From a distance, they cannot be recognized as being either alive or dead. They
have given up eating their rations, knowing and not caring that in so
doing death is imminent.

In Auschwitz, the cell-block chiefs are gods while the traditional
Judaic God is embarrassingly silent. Robert, the sadist block chief
whom Moni later serves as a *Piepel*, enters like a sovereign about to
mount the throne to decree the fate of his subjects:

> Who shall be hung by his writs in the center of the block,
> and who shall get twenty-five in the ass; whose head to
> be shoved into the excrement inside the latrine hole to
> suffocation, and who shall be laid out on the ground to
> be seesawed with a cane across his throat.

Like the God of Israel as envisaged in the *Unetaneh Tokef*, the
prayer used in the liturgy for the High Holy Days, Robert is the sole
master of the fate of those who are unfortunate enough to be placed
under his supervision.[10]

Moni's Piepeldom, like Daniella's prostitution in *House of Dolls*,
represents the novel's greatest moral indictment. Moni's physical
suffering and mental anguish parallel Daniella's. His loyalty to the
Rabbi of Shilov is an expression of the ideals he found in his own
childhood home, for the Rabbi of Shilov is the only person in the
entire book who affirms, however weakly, a dignity and humanity
that is antithetical to Auschwitz life. This is the reason that Fruchenbaum, a Jew who has tried to conceal his identity both the other
Jews and to the Germans, hates the rabbi. But to others, including
Moni, the Rabbi of Shilov offers the following encouragement:
"Life belongs to God. If we willingly walk into the German's fire
we shall be accomplices to the murder."

On Yom Kippur, the Rabbi of Shilov recites the *Unetaneh
Tokef* prayer, thereby affirming what others cruelly deny. When the
pious Haym Idl seeks out the rabbi for his blessing, the rabbi cannot
give his comfort because he is no longer sure of either God's power
or his own power to bestow life and blessing. Moni, a descendant
of the rabbinic aristocracy, is naturally drawn to one who embodies
the values he receives at home before he was caught in the trap of
Auschwitz. Moni, as we have seen, has his mother's black eyes—
"velvet black like Grandpa the rabbi"—and it is through the look in
the eyes of the Rabbi of Shilov that Moni receives the message, "Run
away, Moni!. . .Run for your life." It is the human worth and dignity
that Auschwitz denies which draws Moni to the rabbi; of all the

people in the cell block, it is said of him alone "that he is still human." In Auschwitz, where knee bends are "sport and a sauna is a gas chamber," the Rabbi of Shilov represents the traditional religious values that sustain the child Moni.

Moni himself is unable to betray his heritage. Even when his "paramours" deride him and call him an old whore when they tire of him, he only thinks yearningly of being a little boy again in his mother's arms. Despite the fact that his cell-block Nazi lovers want his flesh to be plump and round so that he can arouse them sexually, his disgust with the role forced upon him destroys his appetite, and as a consequence, he becomes too thin to be a successful *Piepel*. Although he is grateful for the *funktion*—or position—of a *Piepel*, he is the only *Piepel* in the novel who never endangers the life of another. While Lolek takes over Moni's *funktion* as a *Piepel*, leaving him without a job and in danger, he cannot hate Lolek because he dreams that his mother would not like it. He steals only to keep himself alive. Being a *Piepel* hardens him so that he "learn the rules of the game," but he realizes that his weakness is that he is "softhearted." When the Rabbi of Shilov seems to look at him in the same way that his mother did, Moni bursts into tears.

After Moni's conscience kept him from eating, and he became too thin to be a satisfactory *Piepel*, he lost his access to food. When he was a *Piepel*, the sexual subjugation to which he was exposed so revolted him that he could not eat; now starving—like his older brother, Harry—he struggles to maintain his vitality by not becoming a Mussulman. His legs tell him "Moni, you are a Mussulman," and the bones of his legs, indeed, protrude like those on corpses. Having become so emaciated from starvation, Moni tries to talk his way back in a *funktion* as a *Piepel*, which would give him access to food, only to be rebuffed by the retort, "You look beat, old whore."

Like Daniella's, Moni's final escape and death are the climax of the valiant struggle to maintain his human integrity. Fearing the advent of the final pangs of starvation before he becomes a Mussulman and after which hunger will no longer torment him, Moni attempts to make a heroic but futile escape from Auschwitz. Although at the end of the book he dies from hunger and exhaustion, even the Germans, seeing his valiant attempt, nonethless salute him for his effort. Moni, who could neither live in his role as *Piepel* nor forfeit his humanity by becoming a Mussulman, preferred to affirm the value of life by dying rather than submit to a slow, dehumanizing death.

Ka-Tzetnik's most complex work, *Phoenix Over the Galilee*, synthesizes the motifs of his two earlier novels.[11] Like the phoenix,

Harry Preleshnik emerges from the death of Auschwitz reborn into a new life: "Though I said I would die with my nest, I have, like the Phoenix, multiplied my days."[12] The novel's meaning is embedded in the motifs and symbols that the reader can easily miss by becoming engrossed in the deceptively simple narrative line. Beginning in Israel in *media res* with Galilea's going to her psychiatrist for treatment of her obesity caused by the obsessive hatred and fears that she has drawn from Harry, the scene shifts to her childhood and to her earlier life when she is a spirited young woman looking for an ideal lover who embodies the Orthodox Jewish religious ideals of redemption and salvation which she inherited from her father. Ka-Tzetnik then alternates his third-person narration between Harry's release from Auschwitz and Galilea's search for an appropriate mate. By pure chance, she reads a novel of Harry's which describes the terrible happenings at Auschwitz, and she realizes that here is the man she has always sought. At the beginning of their relationship, it is Galilea who provides Harry with the love and strength he needs, but as she learns more and more about the unhealed psychological wounds that he and others carry from their experiences during the Holocaust, she realizes that no one can be redeemed from Auschwitz until the deep emotional scars heal.

When Galilea first meets Harry, she is aware that she knowingly fell in love with a walking corpse:

> It was not in Auschwitz but while still in the ghetto that his soul had been killed. He had passed into the planet Auschwitz a dead man, as other dead men pass into the ultimate unfathomable.

As we have seen in *House of Dolls*, Harry nearly became a Mussulman, but although he became a Mussulman physically, "he had guarded his mind from becoming a Mussulman in spirit." In Israel, Harry struggles with the same life—death dilemma that Moni and Daniella resolved in affirming life by their willingness to die. When in Auschwitz, Harry's body was at death's threshold; and his mind and spirit clung to life; once he is restored to physical health, his mind and spirit seem to have expired. At first, Harry views himself as a blood redeemer, but he realizes that such personal vengeance as he might inflict would be trivial in the face of the crime of genocide that he has to avenge.[13] Aware that when he reaches Israel he is both physically and psychologically without identity, he adopts the name "Phoenix." Having lost everything, even his own name, he no longer feels himself to be a living member of humanity:

Life billowed and splashed around him, his loneliness tossing in it like a dumb pebble. The language men use with one another had dried up in him as though it never had existed. And he, in his own eyes, seemed not to exist.

While the name Phoenix adequately describes his self-image of himself as one who has died and is standing on the threshold of re-birth and new identity, he is distressed by the thought of his own name:

Suddenly he was assaulted by the pain of the name Harry Preleshnik. . . .The name, his very own in the past, was strangling him.

Although he finds comfort in his solitude, Harry still longs to rejoin human society. While he insists on preserving his anonymity, he still wants to be with people, particularly on the Sabbath. His loneliness, a product of the distrust and hatred of the human race which he acquired at Auschwitz, drives him into isolation, but finally the will to live and to love draw him to Galilea, and through her to reconciliation with humanity. When Harry is introduced to Galilea, she recognizes him as the author of a novel about Auschwitz that she greatly admires. Drawn to this man whose book expresses her deeply nationalist and messianic feelings, she wants to cry out his *name*: "Harry Preleshnik." The returning to Harry of his own name is the first step in his psychological rehabilitation.

Ka-Tzetnik traces Harry's development in *Phoenix Over the Galilee* against the backdrop of Galilea's changing demeanor and the static but interpretive motifs of redemptive love and salvation. When at the novel's beginning, Galilea is waiting to see her psychiatrist and while Harry at home is putting their two small children to bed, "black knots of smoke surged back" billowing in her brain. As the novel develops, the reader gradually discovers that Galilea healed Harry by lifting the burden of Auschwitz from him and by taking it upon herself. The madness that he encountered at Auschwitz is assumed by Galilea, driving her to compulsive eating and obesity. In one scene, Ka-Tzetnik effectively contrasts the naked, starved Mussulmen of Auschwitz with a taxi driver's caustic suggestion that Galilea should pay twice because her corpulent body occupies two seats. Similarly, Harry's liberation from Auschwitz is immediately preceded by Galilea's walk and talk with David Artzi, who is her masculine counterpart. The insensitivity of the British and Israelis to the Palestinian Arab populace are suggestive of the Nazi atrocities in callousness if not in magnitude, and Galilea later juxtaposes her inordinate fear of the Germans which she acquired from Harry with her irrational fear of the Fedayeen. All these shifts and juxtapositions underscore the interrelationship between the deaths and hatreds of the past and the need for redemptive love and rebirth.

After David Artzi and Galilea have discussed their inability to find a satisfying love, the narrative moves to David's mission to postwar Europe where he rescues Harry. Like the biblical King David, David Artzi is redheaded.[14] When Harry takes David's place as Galilea's partner, David appears with Masha, a woman who, like Harry, has survived the Holocaust and has come to Israel to live. David and Galilea cannot satisfy each other because they are too similar; they both feel the need to aid and serve those who survived the concentration camps. They are redemptive personalities. Like David, whose surname Artzi means "my land," Galilea's ancestry testifies to her ties to Israel; her father also was one of the founders of the city of Tel Aviv and her own first name suggests the area of Palestine where Jesus, the Christian's Messiah began his ministry, Galilea refers to Israel as the land of Jesus. When working with the Arabs, she is called Geulah, the Hebrew word for redemption. Her birthday is on November 29, which is the date that the United Nations voted to end the British Mandate over Palestine, thus marking the beginning of Israel as an independent Jewish state. Once married, Galilea sets Harry to work writing another book in the same way that in the Talmud, Rachel, the wife of the redheaded messianist, Rabbi Aqiba, sent her husband away so that he might study Torah[15]. Her father rides a donkey, rather than in a Cadillac, emphasizing the messianic quality of his mission.[16]

For Ka-Tzetnik, restitution and redemption can be brought about only by love. What Galilea and Harry both required is love, not pity. The love that Galilea gives to Harry is as redemptive for him as the love that he later returns to her during her illness; once they are restored to health they direct this redemptive love toward the Palestinian Arab community. It must be emphasized, however, that Ka-Tzetnik's vision of the redemptive power of love is neither fanciful nor sentimental. The memorial prayer, *El Maleh Rahamim,* is recited when Harry and Galilea are married; there are memories that cannot be and ought not to be erased. By naming their children Daniella and Monish after Harry's brother and sister, Harry and Galilea preserve their memory.

Although Harry and Galilea heal each other through love, they cannot convince the Jewish and Arab communities to understand one another. For Ka-Tzetnik, it is selfless love that makes redemption a possibility: but nothing is assured and no panacea is offered; the only certainty is that vengeance and hatred solve nothing. Harry is emotionally fulfilled by caring for others. Thus in *Phoenix Over the Galilee*, Ka-Tzetnik's belief that altruistic love is the only possible antidote for fear and hatred is clearly expressed.

Chapter 2

The Psychological Scars of the Holocaust Survivor

Yoram Kaniuk

Yoram Kaniuk's *Adam Resurrected*, like Ka-Tzetnik's *Phoenix Over the Galilee*, depicts the struggle of a Holocaust survivor to overcome the burden of terror and guilt which has overwhelmed him.[17] Ka-Tzetnik, himself a survivor of the death camps, uses events as a major means of communicating his message; Kaniuk, a native-born Israeli who inherited his consciousness of the Holocaust second hand, examines the psychosis of his protagonist whose madness reveals the horror he suffered. Whereas Ka-Tzetnik's immediate experiences can be conveyed through conventional narrative, Kaniuk's vicarious experience is transmitted through the partially coherent confessions and fantasies of a victim.

A psychological novel, *Adam Resurrected* uncovers the thoughts, doubts, impulses and torments of its protagonist, Adam Stein. The narrative line itself is, however, merely a vehicle by which to describe Adam's psychological experiences while in psychiatric treatment. Starting and ending in the home of Ruthie Edelstein, an attractive middle-aged woman who takes lodgers, the novel traces the course of the psychosis that became evident when Adam almost throttled her to death and was, as a consequence, committed to Mrs. Seizling's Institute for mentally disturbed survivors of the Holocaust.[18] It is only through sorting out the unacknowledged passions, fears, and guilts that drove him to attack Ruthie that Adam is able to identify his own being, to return to society, and to become Ruthie's lover.

Adam's schizophrenia stemmed from his assumption of various roles that he found himself forced to play during his struggle for survival during the Holocaust. A clown by profession, Adam used his talents to entertain and pacify Jewish inmates so that they could be exterminated more efficiently. Adam also employed this skill to lure his wife and older sister to their deaths without unnecessary agony. His residual guilt for his deception, coupled with the fact that Commandant Klein at the concentration camp forced Adam to eat out of the bowl reserved for Klein's dog, Rex, drives Adam to project his doubts, fears, and guilts upon a fantasized dog, thus expressing the various interior tensions that Adam himself cannot resolve.

At first, the dog is a demonic double; Adam often refers to the dog as a monster. Still, his projection of Klein and of the doggish personality he assumes as a survival tactic requires that he isolate the animal element within himself in order to overcome the guilt that he bears by having denied his own humanity:

> Look dog. I've been thinking about you. . . .Something tells me you're more than a dog, or less than a dog. . . . You're a human being even if you are a dog.

Once recognized, the fantasized dog represents both human and animal qualities; when Adam realizes that the many tensions surging within him are both animal and human, the dog, at first demonic, becomes a curative force. This demonic monster can also be a "holy tormented saint," an alter ego named Herbert who functions like a brother, and David, King of Israel.

Adam Stein's very name symbolizes the schizophrenic tension inherent in the protagonist. Struggling to be a man, the son of man *Adam ben Adam*, he is also a stone (*stein*) because he is no longer able to love. Sorting out the various aspects of doggishness that afflict him, Adam rediscovers and reclaims himself from the "oblivion of doggishness." By projecting a human and redemptive alter ego on the dog—David, King of Israel—Adam, a man whose adult life has been given to playing roles other than himself in a continuous Purim act, rediscovers his personality which had been submerged for so long by the various alter egos that he had assumed.[19]

Kaniuk does not consider that Adam will ever be completely cured; in the final chapter, a letter to Joseph Graetz, Adam's son-in-law who has married his surviving daughter, Ruth, discloses that Adam has contained his tensions without conquering them. In a post-Holocaust world, a residual neurosis must always linger even after the death camps have long been closed. Adam cannot escape his Holocaust memories; they accompany him constantly. The recreation room at the institute evokes memories of the concentration camp; the institute itself is synthetic and lifeless; it is located in

the desert, which is hot as hell. When Adam escapes from the institute to confront a fantasized Commandant Klein in the desert, he
addresses Klein and the hell he survived with all of its contradictory
ambivalence. In his mirage, he can identify his tormentor, but he is
unable to kill him:

> I know you're a bastard, but I love you. I'll curse you yet
> I'll come to the desert to look for you. We are both lost,
> we have both perished. Our voices are the voices of ghosts.
> Jew to Jew, God to son of God, man to father of man. In
> these synthetic, beheaded days, that is the only dialogue
> that makes sense.

Klein had assumed an alias in order to survive. He had been a
Dr. Weiss who, were it not for the political situation imposed upon
him, would have been a professor of Assyriology. The *whiteness*
(*Weiss*) of his Jewish name was dwarfed by the smallness of his
cowardly and dehumanized alias (Klein). Because Adam can now
distinguish between these qualities in Klein and yet not try to kill
the fantasized Klein, he is able to return to Ruthie.

Just as the emotional paralysis of Adam's ability to love was
caused by life in a concentration camp, so now the curative tendency
within him is recognizable even in his disoriented state. The child
that he envisages in the dog regards Adam as a savior; when the
pious Schwester sisters who are also inmates at the institute view
Adam as a messiah, he names his dog David, King of Israel. Adam
cannot look to God for help because God allowed history's greatest
crime to take place. He must redeem himself because he lacks God.
Realizing that he is not God, he searches for God in Gross, the
institute's director; in the fantasized Klein; and in the fantasized dog
whom he creates and fears. Rex, the dog whose bowl he shared and
with whom he ate, and whom he later emulated, was, is, and will
be the God that takes the place of the God of the normative Jewish
tradition.[20] For Adam in his post-Holocaust nightmare, God can
no longer be the ruler of the universe because God was the architect
of hell.

Adam also must conquer his exploitive, erotic infatuation with
another woman, Jenny Gray, before he can return to Ruthie. Jenny
follows the conventional social rules cruelly and compulsively.
Before she met Adam, she was a virgin, but a virgin out of indiffer-
ence rather than commitment. Adam considers her a whore because
he realizes that her fanatical obsession with rules is really a sublim-
ation of an essentially sinful nature. It is no wonder that her destruc-

tive impulses find a willing object in Adam, for he realizes that she is packed with the "care-free abandon of a crushed sinner." Basically a frigid woman, Jenny is fascinated "with the death implicit in every step" that Adam undertakes. When he feels that his own extinction is imminent, he finds in her a willing partner. Ruthie wants and needs Adam's love and companionship so much that she is even willing to risk her own death at his psychopathic hands; Jenny needs Adam's demonic abandon only to satisfy her own death wish. Once he is healed, Adam returns to Ruthie who, like his dead wife and daughter, represents the humanity and stability that existed in that long-lost time before the rise of Hitler. Significantly, Adam had to leave Ruthie when the monster within him surfaced to attack her. Once that demon has been isolated and overcome, he can return to his devoted, faithful love.

Kaniuk's *Adam Resurrected* is an extremely successful integration of aesthetic and thematic concerns. The problems of the survivor of the Holocaust are made clear without any compromise in artistic standards. The use of a psychotic protagonist who tries to live with the horrors of the past in a godless, rootless culture, and in so doing, regains his sanity, is emblematic of the secular Israeli's response to the death camps.

Abba Kovner

For Abba Kovner, poetry is the one medium through which the Jew may experience, comprehend and conquer the vast enormity of the Holocaust, for it is only in poetry that the categories of life and death are transcended. As Kovner himself has eloquently stated:

> I inherited many things from my ancestors. One is the teaching that a man should not say his prayer before the prayer of the community. . . .But the community in which I pray and say my poems is half alive and half dead. Who are the living and who are the dead? I don't know how to answer this question. But I believe there is one place in the world without cemeteries. This is the place of poetry.[21]

The work of Abba Kovner that most directly focuses on the Holocaust is the long poem, "My Little Sister," which apparently was inspired by a young half-crazed Jewish girl who crawled up over the corpses thrown into the mass-burial pits at Ponar and returned to the Vilna ghetto, some twenty miles distant, where she reported the extinction of some forty thousand persons. In "My Little Sister," Kovner describes in a series of poems divided into five parts the plight of a small Jewish girl who has escaped death at the hands of the Nazis by being placed in a convent, her childishly naive hopes of returning to her family, and her death in the Bikur Holim hospital. Although the fate of the little sister is at the poem's center, this work is also concerned with the relationship between her and her dead brothers, one of whom is the poem's narrator. Speaking from the grave, he mourns the fate that has befallen his sister and, by extension, his own family, his own people, and the world.

> From here the world of the living
> is seen.
> From here a whole world watches
> my face dissolve into
> blue.

From his omniscient perspective, the narrator observes and comments upon the world of those who are still alive, whom he regards as being more dead than he; ironically, the Dominican nuns who give the little sister shelter in the convent also view their guest as "ashes that speak." Whereas her brother-narrator "clings to his flesh as if alive" in death, he mourns the fate of his sister whose lot is worse than his own:

> At the edge of the redeeming pit,
> my sister
> we remembered your going alone.

In death, the narrator need no longer fear the terrors of the Holocaust; his sister, unredeemed by death, suffers loneliness in a life of fancy and isolation.

Kovner's surrealistic technique must be examined in the context of its shifting themes and biblical illusions. In describing the convent's wall that separates the little sister from the world, the narrator writes:

> A cloister's wall is high.
> A wall of silence
> is still higher.
> A ladder leans to the wall.
> Tops of chestnut trees touch and recoil
> from the bell tower.
> Three chestnut trees
> out of a land of lakes
>
> and mud.

Juxtaposing the cloister's physical wall with the walled silence of the dead and risen spirit, Kovner contrasts the opposing forces of the solitude of the afflicted little Jewish girl and the frozen smugness of the community of self-righteous Christians. The first instance of this occurs in the poem's very first stanza, when the frozen ring of the iron chime does "not shake." Affirming the moral value of his own silence, the narrator-poet vows that he will not speak "of a world that went to ruin." The response of silence also stands in opposition to the high moral pretentions of the Church. The phrase "and mud," added after a pause, cancel that soaring of the bell tower by revealing the ugliness and hypocrisy below. Only by silence can the Holocaust victim's moral protest be registered cogently. Consequently, when the little sister is approaching a redeeming death, she is told, "Quiet, quiet"; she will not die with a scream.

"My Little Sister" contains a number of allusions to the Song of Solomon. In the biblical analogue, the lover and the beloved are eventually united; in Kovner's poem, the only resolution that can take place is the silence of death because no earthly union of the sister-bride (*ahoti kala*) and the brother-groom can ever be consummated. When she is not referred to as a bride, the little sister is spoken of as a "fragile sister" (also *ahoti kala*).

Once she is admitted to the convent, the lot of the little sister is steadily contrasted with that of the "nine little sisters" or nuns. When the nine nuns, or sisters (Hebrew has a single word—*ahot*—for both sister and nun), escort the little sister into the convent chapel,

> . . .the son sees
> and the father stares.

Here the allusion is to Jesus, the son, who sees only the acquisition of a new soul to add to the flock of the faithful; whereas God, the father, the patriarchal God of Judaism, stares in silent disapproval. From his omniscient view, the dead poet-narrator comments:

> My sister sits at the window. She
> waits for a brother.

While the little sister futilely waits for her brother to arrive, the nine nuns also are waiting for a man, their "starving eyes ripe with love." The nuns profess a cultic religious chastity, but they have not lost their instinctive sexual desires; their charge, the "little sister, was not introduced to the world." The nine sisters have "such clean hands (Hebrew, *nikyon yadaim*) and pure minds"—a reference to the verse in Psalm 24 that describes those who will, through their merit, ascend the Lord's holy hill:

> He that hath clean hands, and a pure heart;. . .
> Who hath not taken my name in vain,
> And hath not sworn deceitfully.[22]

The sisters' hands may be physically clean, but Kovner artfully avoids any reference to purity in describing the nuns, whose spiritual chasteness, unlike that of their ward, is defiled by sexual longing:

> Night after night
> the Sisters breathe hard in their beds
> as if raised on a ladder.
> Their bodies shake.
> And on this night, too, heavy with longing,
> the gowns on their skins are burning.

A lame nun, whose name is Christina, hopes that she will gain eternal life; in this life she is unfulfilled. A second nun, also named Christina, mistakes the sun's heat for the satisfaction that she longs for when she "labors to sleep." Two other nuns—Irena and Olga—suggestively caress the stone figure of the crucified Jesus, and the little sister's eyes respond:

> Blessed are the crucified,
> thus crucified.[23]

The nuns suffer by choice and are still alive; the little Jewish girl is on death's threshold; her parents and brothers no longer alive, she suffers in a restless wakeful sleep. (Ironically, the stone figure on the crucifix, whom the nine sisters adore, represents one who, like the little sister, suffered in innocence.)

The most revered nun in the convent was once a prostitute, the Hebrew term for which is *kideshah*. This word, in its biblical context, means cult prostitute and is etymologically related to the rabbinic Hebrew term of the maritally licit conjugal relationship, *kiddushin*. Through her marriage to the church she became a cult figure rather than a common whore, her sexual transgressions receiving the pardon of the church because her body is now directed toward a higher end.

The disparity between the nuns' outwardly professed commitment and their actual desires is most blatantly expressed in the following lines:

To give them back
in pity
in open arms
in ringing bells
in blood
Nine sisters drenched with pleasure.
Morning rises
for love
My little sister
is scared.

Unaware of Christendom's sins and moral offenses to the Jews and to the little sister, the insensitive nuns are too preoccupied with their own salvation to bestow any love or Christian charity upon their terrified ward. Overly concerned with their personal fate, they receive pardon for their sins like "whore's pay."[24] While the nuns dream lustfully of their saviour, the fragile sister (*ahoti kala*) is portrayed in bridal imagery, alluding to the sister-bride motif. Both the nuns and the little sister suffer frustration; the nuns because their religion does not permit them the sexual outlet they unconsciously crave; the little sister because her parents, brothers, and community are no longer alive to rescue her or to sanctify her in marriage. In both instances no consummation can take place. In the case of the nuns, their smug, pious delusions betray the spiritual redemption that they seek; in that of the little sister, marriage and maturity are inconceivable. Ironically, the nuns have erotic dreams which their religious vows prohibit; the little sister dreams of being united with her family and becoming a Jewish bride.

After contrasting the little sister's purity with the nuns' lust, the poet-narrator imagines the little sister's wedding day which can never take place. He speaks of his sister sitting at the bridegroom's table from which the groom is absent. "Our father took his bread, baked bless God, forty years from one oven. He never imagined a whole people could rise in the ovens and the world, with God's help, go on." Like bread baked in the oven, European Jewry rose in smoke, the forty years alluding to the years of wandering in the desert after the exodus from Egypt. The absence of further comment is a form of understatement indicating a misplaced faith in Providence, for the bridegroom's voices comes "from the hideout of mourners." Those seated at the table can only reply in impotence:

We will set the table without you;
the marriage contract will be written in stone.

The contract is therefore implicitly a union that will never be consummated because the contract is on the bridegroom's gravestone. Returning to the actual situation of the little sister, the narrator wishfully ponders:

> Blessed be he among men
> who will bring her to his rooms,
> my bridegrooms.

In the Song of Solomon the royal bridegroom escorts his bride to the bridal chamber to consummate their marriage, but for the little sister, such an event is not possible; her bridal bed will be her grave.[25] The white dress that she wears when "her time has come" is a shroud. Unable to help their sister, the dead narrator and his brothers ask collectively:

> What shall we do for our sister
> and she like a wilted tendril.

While the first lines quoted above allude to the wedding day when the sister "will be spoken for,"[26] the second refer to the withered glory of Ephraim which is compared to a wilted tendril.[27] The hope anticipated in the first lines is negated by the cruel reality of the second.

Unlike the other members of her family, the little sister was not put to death, but because of her spiritual isolation, she can never enter into "a covenant of blood" on the day "she will be spoken for"; she will never be able to stand under the traditional Jewish marriage canopy; she must find her consecration in a different fashion:

> behold you
> are consecrated
> more than eagles
> and angels.

The conventional Hebrew formula for betrothal makes the little sister's consecration more tragic.[28] Similarly, the use of the biblical phrase, "from eagles," which is taken from David's lament for Saul and Jonathan and its adaptation in the Hebrew memorial prayer, *Av ha-Rahaman*.[29] intensify her tragic fate. Because she is lost even while she is yet alive, her mother cannot be given comfort for her.[30]

In Kovner's poetry the interregnum between life and death is purposely blurred. By investing the dead with an omniscient consciousness and the living with the helplessness of the dead, he illustrates the ambiguity that confronted displaced post-Holocaust Jewry. Those who survived the Holocaust physically died spiritually, while those who died physically remained and remain very much alive in the memories of the survivors.

Uri Tsvi Greenberg

In Uri Tsvi Greenberg's poems as in Kovner's, the boundaries between life and death have a highly authentic and metaphysical legitimacy. Unlike Kovner, whose poetry is entirely elegiacal and mournful, Greenberg's lament for European Jewry is a summons to revival and rebirth, and thereby associates the Holocaust with the ancient vision of the Covenant and the salvation of the Jewish people. Baruch Kurzweil has aptly stated:

> It appears to me that Uri Tsvi Greenberg is the greatest force in our poetry, not because of his view or his very positive attitude towards Jewish tradition, but rather because Greenberg's texts. . .reveal to me the most focused and interesting portrayal of the internal consistency of our [national-religious] fate.[31]

Greenberg's eschatological vision is an extension of his belief in the traditional religious doctrine of the eternality of Israel.[32] This doctrine appears throughout his Hebrew collection, *Rehovot ha-Nahar.*[33] A study of the English translations of two of the poems from this volume—"We Were Not Likened to Dogs Among the Gentiles" and "Lord! You Saved Me From Ur-Germany as I Fled," illumines this point of view.[34]

Kurzweil has already noted that much of Greenberg's poetry is concerned with opposites or polarities.[35] In "We Were Not Likened to Dogs Among the Gentiles," the poet underscores the disparity between the treatment accorded the Jews and animals, the consequence being that since the Jews were never placed on the same ethical and cultural plane of reference as domestic animals, all the conventions of humaneness that might have applied to them were inapplicable. This thesis is artfully underscored by Greenberg's use of the passive voice:

> We were not likened to dogs among the Gentiles—They pity a dog.
> Caress, even kiss him with the Gentile mouth. For like a puppy
> Fondled at home, they pamper it, delight in it always
> And when this dog dies—how very much the Gentiles mourn him!

In the original Hebrew all the descriptions of how dogs are treated are expressed in the passive voice. The initial comparison (Hebrew, *nidmenu*) indicates that unlike the dog, the Jew is not afforded human kindness. Unfortunately, in the English translation, the verbs are occasionally put in the active voice, whereas in the Hebrew, they are passive. According to the Hebrew version, dogs "are to be pitied" (*yeruham*) and caressed (*yeluttaf*) and kissed (*yenushaq*). The dog is not really the indirect object of the verb "delight"; the dog itself is "a delight," a term that in Hebrew is expressed in passive voice (*hammud*). Consistent with all the affection lavished upon the dog, its death precipitates a period of grief and loss appropriate to the death of a beloved member of the family.

The lines in the next stanza complete the negative analogy. The Jew, like the dog, is passive; unlike the dog, however, the passivity of the Jew is linked with extermination, rather than affection and deference:

> We were not led like sheep to the slaughter in the boxcars
> For like leprous sheep they led us to extinction
> Over the beautiful landscapes of Europe. . . .

Although a dog is given the treatment usually reserved for a member of the family, the Jew is not even afforded as much consideration as that given to sheep when they are being shipped to slaughter. Like a leprous sheep, the Jew becomes the object of disgust and avoidance for whom any humane treatment is inappropriate and repugnant. A sheep is slaughtered for food but is not otherwise violated. Jewry is ineligible for the same consideration:

> Before the slaughter they did not pull out the teeth of
> their sheep;
> They did not strip the wool from their bodies as they did
> to us;
> They did not push the sheep into the fire and make ash of
> the living
> And to scatter the ashes over streams and sewers.

Since there "is no recompense for our disaster," Jewish blood and weeping becomes the new frame of comparison for all inhuman torture and terror:

> He who comes to compare will state: He was tortured like
> a Jew.
> Every fright, every terror, every loneliness, every chagrin,
> Every murmuring, weeping in the world
> He who compares will say: This analogy is of the Jewish
> kind.

The shedding of Jewish blood thus will ever remain an indelible stain upon the culture and conscience of Western civilization. The magnitude of Jewish suffering renders the tortured and the torturer alike immortal because henceforward this becomes the frame of reference for all future human suffering.

The title of Greenberg's poem "Lord! You Saved Me from Ur-Germany as I Fled" alludes to the legend in which Abram was saved by the Lord when he was cast into Chaldees, which was both the birthplace of the first patriarch and the domain of the ancient king Nimrod.[36] Following the rabbinic tradition of equating the place name Ur with fire, the deliverance of Abram from the fire becomes the model for those Jews who escaped the fires of the crematoria and turning to God in prayer, the poet admits that he emerged "whole in body but with my spirit torn." As in "We Were Not Likened to Dogs Among the Gentiles," the extreme cruelty invests the victims with a dubious form of immortality; in this case, that borne of suffering may be transformed into a redemptive force.

> ...To carry that heritage
> Dropped from my martyr's shoulders and to deed the
> future
> My beautiful-portion-in-the-heritage-of-Israel for genera-
> tions
> Till it is brought to the mountain of yearning. . . .

The poet's heritage or inheritance (*yerushah*) requires that he stay alive and become the connecting link between the murdered generation of European Jews and the new nation. Only on "the mountain of yearning" may the speaker unload his burden, for only there will his mission end.

> Lord! I live, from your hand I have strength to live
> On my mourning without its forcing me to perish. . . .

For Greenberg, God's providence is affirmed by the fact that "the enemy did not pass through your land." The fact that the land of Israel was never subjected to Nazi invasion is for him a sign of God's beneficant favor.

His own survival in Palestine widens the poet's historical perspective:

> Each of their burdens slipping as they fell, their blood spilling,
> Pray let us carry on our shoulders with love!. . .

Unlike Abraham, European Jewry perished in the fires, but, like Abraham, the Zionists' return to the ancient homeland represents a fulfillment of God's ancient covenant. The torn soul in the first stanza still has the need to mourn as well as to live. For post-Holocaust Jewry, the will to live becomes a Divine imperative with a national mission and redemptive possibilities.

Natan Alterman

The poet Natan Alterman, unlike Uri Tsvi Greenberg, treats the Holocaust as a failure of the Divine power to act in history. Unlike Greenberg, who with all his modernist poetics and willingness to challenge God for not keeping his chosen people from slaughter, cannot break with the classic Jewish doctrines of redemption and salvation, Alterman indicts a god who absents himself from history and thus makes a fundamental break with his more traditional literary antecedents. Alterman's poem "From All Peoples" is actually more an indictment of God's powerlessness than of Nazi brutality:[37]

> When our children cried in the shadow of the gallows,
> We never heard the world's anger;
> For Thou didst choose us from all peoples,
> Thou didst love us and favor us.

By opening with the classical liturgical passage about God's having selected the children of Israel as his chosen people, Alterman underscores the ironic quality of God's having chosen the people of Israel for suffering.[38] The recurring phrase "Thou didst choose us" is used as both a challenge and an indictment each time it appears. After reminding God that he chose the people of Israel over Norwegians, Czechs, or Britons, Alterman notes that the Jewish children are exceptional only insofar as they are aware of their imminent deaths:

> They know that their blood is not counted in the
> bloodshed—

> They only call back to their mothers: "Mother, don't
> look!"

The children call to their mothers and to their God; they ask their mothers to avert their eyes and not look upon them in death because like their fathers they are continuing a tradition of martyrdom:

> Veterans we are, soldiers renowned—
> Only undersized!

Like their forefathers, too, they call upon their ancestral God:

> God of the patriarchs! We know
> That Thou didst choose us from all children,
> That Thous didst love us, and favor us.
> That Thou didst choose us from all children.

After having appealed to God, they then affirm the particular knowledge that made them wise. This knowledge is contained in the anaphoristic exploitation of the liturgical formula concerning the chosen quality of the people of Israel. Standing at the foot of the gallows, the children alter the phrase "from all peoples" to "from all children," thereby expressing a tension that continues to grow until the ironic dimension of Israel's fate indicts their God and His betrayal:

> To be slaughtered before the Throne of Glory;
> And Thou dost gather our blood in buckets
> For there is no one else to gather it.

The slaughter of Israel before "the Throne of Glory" is described in ironic liturgical imagery. In ancient times, once a sacrifice offered, it was required that the blood of the offering be gathered and sprinkled at the base of the altar.[39] Significantly, this is the requirement for the biblical peace offering. Because, during the Holocaust, Israel's children have become God's peace offering, there is no one left to continue the sacrificial service:

> And Thou dost gather our blood in buckets
> For there is no one else to gather it.

As a consequence of the Divine inactivity,

And Thou dost scent it like the perfume of flowers,
And dost sponge it up in a kerchief;
And Thou will seek it from the hands of them that
   murdered
And from the hands of those that kept silent.

In those lines where Alterman depicts God engaged in the grotesque activity of sponging up the spilled blood of his sacrificial victims, the Hebrew phrases all begin with the word *ve-Atah* (and Thou), thereby indicating that the children are impatient in death for God to bring those guilty to account. The challenge "and Thou" finally ends when the children state that those who remained silent must be judged, for ironically, God himself was also silent; the responsibility for the Holocaust is His.

Dan Pagis

Having himself personally experienced life in a concentration camp, Dan Pagis—like Abba Kovner—writes about the Holocaust in a very intimate, immediate way. Whereas Uri Tzvi Greenberg and Natan Alterman propound larger questions, Pagis's poetry is quiet, subtle, and suggestive. In "Testimony," Pagis opens with a mode of defense of his murderers' humanity, and concludes with a denial of God's divinity:[40]

> No no: they definitely were
> human beings: uniforms, boots.
> How to explain? They were created
> in the image.

Unable to deny the humanity of his assailants, Pagis notes that they were created "in the image." (The Hebrew word *bi-tselem* refers to man's having been created in God's image.[41]) The image of man that appears here is anything but human—the human beings created in God's image consist merely of uniforms and boots. Ironically, the "image of God," initially the hallmark of humanity, emerges as a dehumanizing force. Pagis is unable to accept a deity in whose image his murderers were created:

> I was a shade
> A different creator made me.

If the humanity of the Germans is expressed by their corporal presence and their garb, the now disembodied poet must have been made by a different creator, his humanity must have derived from another source:

> And he in his mercy left nothing of me that would die.
> And I fled to him, rose weightless, blue,
> forgiving—I would even say: apologizing—
> smoke to omnipotent smoke
> without image or likeness.

God's mercy as creator is so limited that he has left his follower with nothing mortal. After the poet-speaker ascends to his creator, he apologizes, but it is difficult for the reader to determine to whom the apology is offered. The phrase "smoke to omnipotent smoke" is reminiscent of the biblical sentence meted out to Adam: "You are dust and to dust you will return."[42] The poet is returning to a deity who has neither form nor likeness. According to Maimonides' articles of faith, God has no form or likeness because he is in no way corporeal.[43] In the biblical context, man's uniqueness derives from his having been created in the image of God. By ironically juxtaposing the two doctrines, Pagis suggests that man's inhumanity derives from God's lack of image or likeness; he is as impotent as formless smoke. God, the Germans, and the Jewish poet have all lost their identity as a consequence of the Holocaust; God, because man can no longer have an image of God as a model; the Nazis because they are uniforms and boots without souls; and the Jewish poet because he is now only a shade.

For Pagis, the Holocaust denies the promise of life and humanity. In "Written in Pencil in the Sealed Railway Car," the poet reads a note scratched in pencil that represents humanity's indictment of itself:[44]

> here in this carload
> i am eve
> with abel my son.
>
> if you see my other son
> cain son of man
> tell him i

Havvah, the Hebrew for Eve, means life, and *Hevel*, the Hebrew for Abel, means spirit, blowing wind, or nothingness.[45] For Eve, the mother of all human life, there was now a single son, Abel, from whom nothing came, because he was slain by his brother. Cain, the fratricidal killer, is not present. Eve only asks the reader to "tell him i." The lines are not punctuated because there can be no punctuation for an unreal relationship. The living son of Adam and Eve is Cain; the dead son is Abel, riding with his mother in a railway car on their way to a death camp. Cain is not present, for a murderous mankind kills the very source of life. Eve's only wish is to be recognized as an existent being.

In both poems, Pagis suggests that the Holocaust has robbed humanity of its life and source of being. In an era when relationships no longer obtain and ancient ethical values have been abandoned, a dehumanized mankind must search in vain for meaning and purpose.

T. Carmi

T. Carmi's "René's Songs" presents the longings of a little boy who survived the Holocaust to accept, and be accepted by, the director of the orphanage in which he is now housed.[46] The first stanza portrays the child's alienation and distance from *Lo-Imi*, the name he gives to the woman who is the head of the orphanage:[47]

> Bright-haired am I my face and body white.
> Bright as my mother's hair;
> White as my father's silence;
> The day he ascended in the smoky chariots,
> Why did Lo-Imi whisper in the frosty light that hour!
> —René, you are the black flower.[48]

René is a black flower because of his past experience in a concentration camp. While his life is no longer in physical danger, the hell from which he has emerged has left its residue:

> In my lungs, the blood lurks
> For the frost's white, the sheet's white,
> Decay gnaws my teeth—
> Is that why?

Unable to understand why he is categorized as a black flower, he still feels that the gnawing within him is perceptible to the directress. The recurring refrain "Is that why?" appears four times in the first song, each time when the child has to face the cruel reality that he is irrefutably an orphan.

In the second song, René imagines that his parents are alive and calling him, beckoning him to join them in heaven. Finally, in the third and concluding song, it is spring, and the child turns to addressing the directress directly and happily, as though she were, indeed, his mother:

> Lo-Imi, Lo-Imi!
> From the garden I call you
> I stand by the bamboo tree.
> Please come to the veranda to see the bud.

In a series of lyrical visions, the spring has come, the cold has gone, and those who were ill are healed by a melody that contains a thrice-recurrent refrain: "There are no black flowers,"—a sentence that announces René's redemptive return to life and his acceptance of his present situation:

> When the shining bud sings
> I fasten my mouth
> To the pipe
> and spring melodies break forth and rise
> Out of this damaged lung of mine
> From between my decaying teeth—
> My mother! My mother!
> Like the almond tree I burst in Spring's heart,
> Into the heart of Springtime with lively pipes.

> There are no black flowers!

Once René is able to realize that there can be new life and rebirth he is no longer a black flower, the directress can become a surrogate mother. According to the prophet Hosea,[49] God rejected Israel and called her *Lo Ami* (not my people); with reconciliation, Israel once again becomes *Ami*, or God's people. When René is no longer a black flower, he too can be redeemed by finding a new mother.

Aharon Appelfeld

Aharon Appelfeld, who survived the Holocaust by hiding in a monastery, uses his experience to provide the psychological setting for his introspective fiction, in which he examines the residual effect of the Holocaust on its survivors. According to Leon J. Yudkin, "Appelfeld's subject is. . .the Jewish condition with specific reference to immediate past history as living in the present."[50] Unlike Kovner, Carmi, Greenberg, Pagis, and Ka-Tzetnik, Appelfeld does not write directly about the Holocaust; he creates a fiction in which the Holocaust experience permeates the post-Holocaust setting with a numinous dread that is ever present but only occasionally acknowledged. For S. Kremmer, "the subject of the Holocaust does not come up in the stories,—only the vision of it."[51] In his short story "Bertha," Appelfeld provides the reader with a deceptively simple tale in which the psychological havoc of the unmentioned but obvious past erupts and wreaks continued tragedy upon the story's main characters.[52]

The ostensible hero, Max Schatz, brought Bertha, an autistic or retarded girl, with him as his ward to Palestine after they escaped from the Germans during World War II. At first glance, Max seems the strongest character in the story. He leaves and returns to Bertha at his pleasure and he indicates acquaintanceships with other people while Bertha is fixed in space and time without any other social ties or relationships. Furthermore, Max seems to be able to manipulate Bertha emotionally. A closer examination of the story's structure and themes reveals, however, that actually it is Max who is the passive character and that Bertha is, for him, the source of an unresolved and unresolvable emotional conflict. Her presence prevents Max from having a permanent relationship with Mitzi, an attractive woman whom he meets at work. Mitzi and Bertha represent two opposing polarities between which Max must choose; his very inability to make the choice testifies to his indecisiveness and passivity. Unable to control the reactions of women, Max can only respond. He is unable to change Bertha's situation.

> Inside, in the small room, life remained unchanged. Bertha would sit on the floor, knitting. It seemed as if the passing years did not touch her. She remained just as he had left her in the summer, small, dwarfish. . .unaltered.

While Max believes he is able to move freely and change in space and time, he also believes that Bertha is fixed in the frozen world of the past and her own fantasy. To the same extent that he moves in an outside world, Max is also subject to aging; Bertha, on the other hand, was apparently frozen as a child, not subject to movement and change. Her fantasies replace the events that she does not experience; "The gaps which he had left between the stories provided her with food for fantasy with which to amuse herself." Her childish fantasies do not recognize time or change, but this does not mean that she is passive, or for that matter, that Max is active. Bertha's apparent inactivity is really the result of her stifling plight, which on occasion Max is partially able to recognize:

> Bertha would stand up, looking at him helplessly with her big eyes unable to understand. When he nagged her, she would burst into tears. . . .It wasn't she that wept, some sleeping animal wept inside her.

While Bertha seemed to Max to drag after him like a "dead weight," with a loyalty "that was not quite human," he himself is conscious of the "whole weight of this human burden thrust upon him." Bertha, as a youthful survivor of the Holocaust, is unable to react because there is something frozen, that needs to be thawed, inside her. Max, on the other hand, watches her "as if he was observing his own life." It is Bertha, who to Max represents the Holocaust, who is the source of his ambivalence. He longs to be rid of her, but she is too much a part of him.

When Max leaves Bertha in the winter to work in a beer distribution center, he meets the second woman in his life—Mitzi—who suggests that he institutionalize Bertha. Being attracted to Max, she necessarily views Bertha as a hindrance and even perhaps as competition. Still, as much as Max would like to be free of Bertha, especially when he is being offered the possibility of having a sustained sexual relationship with a mature woman, he is unable to act decisively. He cannot even bring himself to admit that Bertha is retarded. Bertha's stubborn devotion to Max makes him, as her guardian, incapable of casting her off in favor of a relationship with another woman.

Actually, Max's problem is not Bertha at all; it is his own ambivalence toward the past and his own psychological impotence. He is not really close to either Bertha or Mitzi. When he is with Bertha, he nags at her with questions that he knows cannot be answered. Conversely, when Mitzi questions him concerning their possible future together, he is unable to answer. Hence, Max is as uncomfortable with Mitzi's questions as Bertha is with his. In their relationships with Max, both Mitzi and Bertha are covertly active and overtly passive. In the same way that Bertha makes no formal demands of Max, Mitzi never really asks him to institutionalize Bertha. Once Mitzi has attracted Max to her, he suggests, on his own, that he go to the foreman to ask for a leave of absence "to finish once and for all, to get rid of the nuisance." Significantly, Max does not state his intentions explicitly because his remark only reflects wishful thinking. Mitzi's refusal to accompany him when he goes to institutionalize Bertha only increases his confusion. She lacks the unchanging loyalty and devotion that he finds in Bertha. She is as faithless to him as he is to Bertha. Once Max is in the presence of Bertha, "his head was empty of all thoughts. He wasn't sure for what he had come."

His inability to think demonstrates his need for Bertha; should Mitzi betray him after he has institutionalized Bertha, he would be left without companionship. When in the company of the retarded Bertha, Max is unable to think. Once free of Mitzi, Max falls under Bertha's influence. His initial remarks to her upon his return show how much he really needs her:

> "Bertha," he said. It was the biggest word that he could cut out of his heart; it seemed that only once he had called her that way. . . ."I came early this time."

Suddenly aware that she has matured in his absence and how much he needs her, Max becomes the supplicant; Bertha no longer needs nor wants Max. Once Max, in an ineffectual attempt to speak rationally, tries to explain to Bertha that he did not really love Mitzi, the now perceptive Bertha stops him. At the moment when Max comes to realize how much he needs Bertha, she matures and no longer needs him. At the story's beginning, Bertha is repugnant to Max; once she is mature, Max needs her but she no longer wants or needs him. Max's ambivalence derives from the fact that he was too much a part of human society to tolerate Bertha, but he was too tied to Bertha to react well with his peers.

It is significant that although the story is entitled "Bertha," and narrated largely from Max's point of view, for the reader is at first led to believe that Max is active while Bertha is frozen in her world of youthful immaturity. When Max insists on going out without Bertha, the English translation reads "in the evening he managed *to get away*." The term used in the original Hebrew, however, is *li-himalet*, which is an infinitive of the *nif'al* passive construction. Similarly, the English "he managed" is expressed in Hebrew in the passive voice, *nimtze'ah lo*. Translated literally, the text reads "a way of escape was found for him." Unlike either Bertha or Mitzi, Max is very indecisive; when confronted with a challenge he is unable to take any initiative whatsoever.

The relative activity or passivity of the characters is also made clear through the use of symbolic language. References to cold and warm, light and dark pervade the narrative as the story line unfolds. Max has little to say to Bertha because "what had happened had frozen somewhere on the way"; Bertha's room is dark, the light only enters when Max, returning, opens the door. Bertha's private world needs light in order to develop; when Max enters, the reader is told that Bertha "had waited for this light." Because of her helplessness, her "darkness" makes her "gaze fall on him helplessly." When Max comes back after being away with Mitzi and brings into the house with him the cold wintry outside air, Bertha lights the stove. It is Max who freezes Bertha, and it is Bertha who tries to create warmth. He refuses to take her with him, he locks her in the house, and at the story's end, he tries to institutionalize her. While Max, seemingly intentionally, tries to keep Bertha in her fixed state, "he couldn't throw her into the snow." He does not keep Bertha out of altruism—he is by nature a cold person, one who is attracted to the snow: "He conjured up the snow, those thick flakes falling from the skies, soft as a caress." And it is this coolness that Max imposes upon Bertha: "From the day they had reached this country, oblivion had overcome her. Her memory froze at a certain point. . . .Some pipe is stopped up." Once Bertha's memory froze, she became fixed in time until her physical development. Unable to give her the warmth she needs, Max simply leaves her alone in the house. His inability to help her derives from his own ambivalence toward his need for warmth and cold. When he discusses his plans with Bertha, he does so "half maliciously, half affectionately."

Max's ambivalence is also reflected in his inability to institutionalize Bertha. Needing a woman's warmth, he realizes how much he needs her once she has begun to mature physically. Bertha literally craves the warmth that Max is unable to provide. When she mentions that the sun is good, Max can only reply, "It is beautiful." For the most part, he pities her; but his personality is such that he can only "love a little." Now that she has become pubescent, she is warm without Max. He needs her more than she needs the liberating warmth and light that for so long he had denied her.

Realizing that Max had "frozen" her into her autistic state, Bertha now arranges for her own institutionalization. While her new maturity brings her warmth, it also destroys. Her summer dreams of childhood filled the void left by Max's insensitivity until her natural development redeems her with sexuality and death: "A smile lit up in Bertha's face, and there was something sharp in her eyes like an inanimate object slowly changing its form. Darkness rose in the streets, and above them was light."

The light above parallels the darkness within Bertha which was released along with the warmth that burns in her cheeks. Once institutionalized, she feels that her lot is lighter; she is now forever free of Max. On the other hand, some outside force made Max "walk heavier" once she was gone.

In Appelfeld's view, the vast enormity of the Holocaust froze something in Max, who projected this upon Bertha, attempting to keep her in a psychologically frozen state. Unable to recognize the fixity he imposes on Bertha, he is able to appreciate her growth only when he is about to lose her. Appelfeld in no way is preaching directly about the Holocaust; his focus is upon the subtle but residual horror that torments the survivors. Highly personal in scope, his view of the Holocaust is nonetheless remarkably universal. Although ostensibly he examines the microcosm of a disturbed girl's maturation, he actually has written a story about redemption. Max escaped from the Holocaust physically, but the indelible psychological scars he bears, he inflicts upon Bertha. His physical escape with its sense of guilt causes him to stultify Bertha, who needs and craves psychological rebirth. Unable to gain freedom in life, Bertha in turn, condemns Max to his own frozen ambivalence.

Haim Gouri

Haim Gouri's novel, *The Chocolate Deal,* shares certain similarities with Appelfeld's short story, "Bertha," and Kaniuk's novel, *Adam Resurrected.*[53] Through the device of interior monologue, which allows the characters to confess their fears, aims, and drives, he has created a psychological novel that without moralizing has deep overtones. Beginning with the unexpected reunion of Mordi (Mordecai) Neuberg, and Rubi (Reuben) Krauss, *The Chocolate Deal* presents an interlocking series of first-person narratives that display the characters' moral stances in an unnamed war-ravaged European city. Once Mordi, whose name in itself is suggestive of death (*mort*), has succumbed to the death that he anticipated, the conniving, amoral Rubi decides to become rich by creating a fraudulent "chocolate deal" by falsely creating a black-market operation concerning the worth of surplus military chocolate. The initial stark juxtaposition of the characters Mordi and Rubi creates both the ethical and artistic tensions of the novel; according to Robert Alter, "the sketchy action. . .constitutes moral ambiguities of survival."[54]

Mordi, whom Rudi often speaks of as a good boy, or as a little boy, is so morally sensitive to his people's fate that he is wholly passive and impotent. He first appears unnamed; he also feels that he does not deserve to live after his talented friend Moshko was killed; he even convinces himself that he is the "disease" that keeps Rubi from finding wealth and success. As Rubi states with insight, "You want me to plead before you, to repeat that you're a good fellow, a bit too sensitive, that you look into things too much."

Mordi's thoughts are preoccupied with the past, with moral decisions that were and are beyond his power to resolve, as well as with his own approaching death. He notices when Rubi sighs, not realizing that Rubi is whimsically remembering past better days when he was with Gerti, his mistress; Mordi feels more and more guilty that he is alive when his brilliant friend Moshko died; and he even deflects Rudi from engaging in the latter's black-market activities without either of them being able to explain why. After thinking about soldiers who are singing, after having "chests full of medals for heroism, rescue, and death," Rudi notes,

> Mordi has his own brand of patience. He doesn't hurry. Where should he hurry to? He has time. Occasionally Rubi reads frightful ideas on his face. When they go beyond what's permissible, when Mordi looks lost in a long dream, Rubi cries out, "Mordi!" And, like a man waking up, he returns, from his distances, only to smile.

Rubi never consciously understands Mordi's patience or his preoccupation with death and destruction. Unable to withstand the claims that Mordi awakens in him, he yet feels guilty when he is away from him with Gerti; he cannot bear to hear Mordi's moral self-deprecation. For one as morally insensitive as Rubi, "It's hard to figure Mordi out. He's a strange boy. Unpermissibly sensitive to those who are stubborn about living no matter what." Unable to live "no matter what," Mordi dies when Rubi leaves him for a period with Gerti that extends for at least two weeks.

Mordi dies because he cannot bear to live in a brutal and insensitive world. Rubi's hardihood and his willingness to exploit the post-Holocaust world parallel Mordi's preoccupation with death. Rubi wants to find one of his surviving relatives, Dr. Salomon, for his own ends. Unable to make moral distinctions or to die like Mordi, he decides to continue living by parasitically exploiting his few remaining contacts.

Although Rubi is far more aware of the ruined amoral world of which he is a part than Mordi ever was, he is nonetheless now unable to forge his way and gain his fortune. Earlier, talking to Rubi of his life during the war, Mordi mentioned a watchmaker called Schecter who had housed him. At the novel's conclusion, Mr. Schecter appears to the ragged weeping figure of Rubi who is mourning for himself and Mordi at Mordi's grave. The appearance of Schecter, whose name in Yiddish means "slaughterer," symbolizes Rubi's end and fate as much as it does Mordi's. The lives and deaths of both Mordi and

Rubi were senseless tragedies; Mordi's very living was so extreme that he was unable to forget the past and accept the present and it killed him. Rubi's longing for worldly success and security drove him to seek a future that he could not find. In death Mordi preserved his integrity; in life Rubi bartered his away. As a consequence, neither survived their remembrance of the Holocaust experience. In the post-Holocaust era, one may preserve either one's soul or one's life. To preserve both is no longer possible.

Chapter 3

The Second Generation:
The Israeli Search for a
Post-Holocaust Identity

Dahn Ben Amotz

In *To Remember, To Forget* Dahn Ben Amotz describes Uri
Lam's latent fears about the Holocaust and his Jewish identity.[55]
Having escaped from Europe to Israel, Uri finds it necessary to forget
what had happened to him and to his family in Germany; that act of
forgetting continues to bother him until he decides to return to
Germany, and claim reparations for what was done to his parents. By
pressing his claims, Uri also discovers what he has been trying to
forget in the interim between his boyhood escape and his adult
return to Germany, the land of his birth. Once he has reconciled
himself to what has happened and to never seeing his brother Martin
again, Uri hopes to return to Israel a mature man.

Uri's reconciliation with the past is further complicated by the
fact that while he is in Germany he falls in love with Barbara Stahl,
a young German woman whom he eventually marries. *To Remember,
To Forget* is not only a novel about the redemption of an Israeli Jew;
it also portrays that segment of German society which stood idly
by while the Jewish community was annihilated. Only through the
love and support of Barbara does Uri eventually learn to cope with
his own Jewish identity.[56]

Initially reluctant to claim reparations, Uri soon alters his view
and persuades himself that he has every right to be paid for the
horrors inflicted upon his family. Actually it is when his need for a
larger house and better living standards outstrips his income that he
decides to request reparations as payment for his "just and ethical
demands." Feeling guilty about his change of heart, he assumes the
role of a conceited, talkative, and talented young man who lives for

the moment while deluding himself that he is a pragmatist. As the novel progresses, Barbara, a young woman who is sufficiently mature to appreciate Uri's strengths, discovers the true Uri hidden behind this defensive facade which he erected during his years of forgetting. Through his love for his German wife, Uri learns to respect his Jewish self. Just as he was sent off to Palestine from Germany, his return to Germany and his love for a German woman redeem him from the matrix of fear and guilt that compelled him to interpose a facade between himself and others rather than present the authentic Uri Lam.

Even though he convinces himself that his claims for reparations are justified, Uri realizes that his motives are flawed. He is therefore reluctant to admit that his real purpose in coming to Germany is the extraction of blood money as reparation for sufferings he did not himself endure. This ambivalence continues even after he gains a reparation settlement, for Barbara has to convince him that it is proper for him to cash his reparation checks. Uri is also hesitant to tell an official his real name is Lampel. On changing his surname from Lampel to Lam and his first name from Hirsch to Tzvi and then to Uri, he is in effect trying to deny his Jewish identity; but in asking for reparations, it becomes necessary for Uri to identify himself. Only through a confrontation with the authentic self that he has been trying to deny is a true accommodation and reconciliation with the past possible.

Having met Barbara, Uri learns that putting on a false front is no cure for his complicated emotional evasions. Applying fanciful logic, he believes that Barbara does not respect him because he is a Jew. He cannot realize that she loves him as a person while objecting to his erratic behavior. His illogical fears are couched in a defensive logic, but Barbara's mature devotion enables him to confront his Jewishness and, more important, himself.

Uri often finds respite from his fears by entering a world of fanciful imagination. On his initial train ride from Genoa to Frankfurt, he conjures up an escapist vision of Europe as a place of sex and drink. His subconscious fears then bring him to believe that all the Germans on the train are Nazis, only to find that he is sitting next to a homosexual German-Jewish dressmaker whose name is the same as his lost brother's—Martin. Uri's search for his brother is really a search for himself; the homosexual Martin serves as an alter ego for Uri, emphasizing all that is unnatural and deviant in Uri's denial. Uri's desire to deny his identity is poignantly described when he burns the photographs of his German youth, when he officially changes his name, and when he denies his German origins by claiming that he was born in Tel Aviv. He tells his German-Jewish host, Mati, that he has come to Europe to do research because he is too embarrassed to admit the true reason for his journey. Mati then castigates those Jews who, like Uri, have come to Germany for reparations that will enable them to forget what was done in the concentration camps. Unable or unwilling to suffer Mati's pointed rebuke, Uri escapes into sleep.

The longer Uri and Barbara are together, the less he is able to have fanciful visions. He can no longer imagine that Mr. Stahl, Barbara's father, is really a Nazi. Once forced to address people as they are, without the artificial mediation of playing a defensive role, Uri discovers that Mr. Stahl feels guilty because he did not protest when an old acquaintance, a Jewish clockmaker, was taken by the Nazis. When Uri confronts reality directly, he learns that Germans can be humane as well as barbaric.

Uri's ultimate salvation comes after he dons his last disguise, the costume of an ultra-Orthodox Jew, and at Barbara's behest attends an exclusive masquerade ball for the Frankfurt elite. Whereas in all his other encounters throughout the course of the novel, Uri tries originally to hide his racial identity, he now blatantly affirms it. Previously, he has been unable to address his German-Jewish background; his final masquerade enables him to address German society as a Jew, and in so doing, he no longer needs to forget or deny his heritage. Those assembled at the party consider his costume to be offensive because it reminds them of what they would like to forget. Although no one comments that Martin's Nazi costume is in bad taste, they stand in mute dismay when a prearranged skit is performed in which the homosexual Nazi, Martin, orders the Jew, Uri, to leave the party. In this skit, Uri and Martin remind the Germans of what they would like to forget—that their residual anti-Semitism is yet to be acknowledged and conquered. By reminding the Germans of their anti-Semitism, Uri exacts his revenge without exploiting or commercializing his parents' memory. The reparation payment is no longer blood money that cancels a debt; it simply represents the inheritance that is due.

The two motifs that accompany Uri's redemptive catharsis are Barbara's love and reconciliation. Uri marries a Christian woman, even though in so doing he offends traditional Jewish sensibilities. Once, walking down a hill as though it was the Via Dolorosa, he asks himself why he is walking like a "crucified Christ." Throughout the novel, Uri has been a Judas-like figure who has denied his identity, but by bearing his identity like an atoning cross, he discovers the meaning of his Judaism through his Christian love, Barbara.[57]

This redemptive self-awareness is only possible after Uri learns to curb his compulsive tongue. He insults Mr. Stahl by talking too much; he is abusive to the people who bought the house in which he was born; a drunken tirade against the Nazis precipitates an altercation in which he is beaten by local thugs. Significantly, his last audacious act does not require him to say anything. By simply *acting* as a Jew, he overcomes his excessive talking. This habit of excessive talk is closely linked to Uri's identity conflict. Through talk, he can deny who he is. It is interesting to note that Barbara is first attracted to Uri in the broken elevator when they first meet because Uri, feigning no knowledge of German, is unable to speak. Once married, Barbara is fearful of Uri's "excessive talking." Once Uri's confrontation with his past is complete, he no longer talks excessively. He returns to Israel, reconciled to both the Jewish and German dimensions within himself and resolves to live his life facing his past and present with his German Gentile wife.

Yehuda Amichai

Like Dahn Ben Amotz's *To Remember, To Forget*, Yehuda Amichai's *Not of This Time, Not of This Place* is a psychological novel in which the hero tries to confront and reconcile the haunting past of the Holocaust.[58] According to Leon Yudkin, the book represents

> a character at a decisive moment in his life, who splits into two parts, one of which stays in Jerusalem where the action is first located, and one of which goes back to the town of his birth, Weinburg, Germany.[59]

This summary of the plot is essentially correct. The novel does indeed trace the troubles and undisciplined stream of consciousness of Joel, a talented but disoriented young archaeologist. Born in Germany and sent to Palestine in his youth, Joel fantasizes a trip to Germany so that he might learn about little Ruth, his childhood sweetheart, and avenge her death. His daydreams about Germany are relayed to the reader through his unreliable first-person narrative, but those events that take place in Israel are presented in the third person. The disparity between the two alternating narratives is one of perception; throughout the novel both the daydreams and realistic narration deal with the same themes, but the isolation of Joel's unreliable first person narration enables the reader to observe Joel's growing disorientation which severs Joel's ties with reality and ultimately precipitates his death. In the third-person narration, Joel is unfaithful to his wife, Ruth, while he shares an apartment with

Patricia, an American Gentile who is working as a nurse in Jerusalem. Joel's actual infidelity to his wife is paralleled by his imagined infidelity to his childhood sweetheart, little Ruth, when he becomes infatuated with Leonore, an assimilated Israeli emigrée who has rejected her ethnic and family ties. While Joel never considers his attraction to Leonore as faithlessness, his attraction to her seductive body at a tennis match occasions the loss of the artificial leg that might have belonged to little Ruth.

Joel's infidelity is accompanied by a compulsive death wish. During his journey to Germany, he finds a German Jewry that either has died in the war or is about to die. The death of Rabbi Manheim, little Ruth's father, occurs in the third-person narrative on the same day that Henrietta dies in Joel's unreliable stream of consciousness. His search for his childhood sweetheart is also a search for death. He goes to Germany to "be with his dead little Ruth." Joel's remark is intentionally ambiguous when understood in the context of his interest in death. It is not clear whether he wants to be with Ruth or whether he simply wants to die. Mina, a flirtatious and adulterously inclined woman who, like Joel, is psychologically unbalanced, advises him to get involved "with things that don't exist anymore."

Throughout the novel, Joel learns of many deaths. As we have noted above, Rabbi Manheim dies on the same day that Joel learns of Henrietta's death. Mina links Joel's interest in archaeology with his interest in the dead. Archaeology is a "science that thrives on wars and the dead," she comments, and she notes that Joel is concerned with "jars and more jars and scrolls and bits and pieces and some ashes and scraps and heads with chipped noses. That's all. That's your entire world." Her observation emphasizes the pointlessness and triviality of Joel's life search, which ultimately ends in a confrontation with the dead and broken. In Joel's final fantasy, either at the moment of death or perhaps after it, he muses,

> As I sat in the small peaceful square in Paris at the end of the summer, a great forgetfulness descended upon me like grace. This beautiful city was the last stop on my journey. It seemed to me that I had already died and I was in a different world.

Once Joel passes through doors that bear the inscription, "Outsiders not allowed," he sees the totality of his life from beginning to end "shrouded in mist."

Joel's death wish ultimately leads him back to Patricia. Significantly, he now prefers to call her Patrice, the French form of her name, for when in Paris, his mind dies. When aroused, Patricia's lips tremble with a fear of death. Her husband, Melvin, considers her to be an uncontrollable destructive child. It is through Patricia that Joel finds a goddess of death whom he worships with sex. Like the faithless Mina, who often walks barefoot, Patricia is regularly seen walking stockingless and barefoot with her thighs suggestively exposed. She removes her shoes before making love and Joel, when he hears the sound of her bare feet on the floor, becomes sexually aroused.

This obsession with death and its priestess, Patricia, is couched in cultic terminology. Through Patricia, Joel tries to find a substitute for his memories of little Ruth and for the teachings of her father, the liberal Orthodox rabbi of Weinburg:

> The Reverend Patricia, a preacher like Rabbi Dr. Manheim. I love you.

Joel remembers having been impressed with the liturgy of the High Holy Days, especially the prostration ceremony on the Day of Atonement. It is interesting that this is juxtaposed with a visit to a confessional booth. When Melvin discusses his marital problems with Joel in the first-person narration, Joel mutters, "Our Father, Our King," a phrase taken from that liturgy.[60] When in the company of Sybil, a girl who reminds Joel of little Ruth and who has a part in a movie that is being made dealing with the destruction of Weinburg, he thinks of the shofar, the ram's horn, that is sounded in the synagogue on Rosh Hashanah and at the conclusion of Yom Kippur. Underlying all this cultic imagery is the theme of vengeance as a form of atonement. Joel thinks of the bombing of Weinburg as fitting revenge against the population of his native city which allowed little Ruth to be killed. Just as Joel is preoccupied with the dichotomy between vengeance and atonement, he longs to reconcile Eros, as exemplified by Patricia and Thanatos, the fate of the family and of the ethical and moral teachings of Rabbi Manheim.

Joel's real crisis derives from his guilt at having escaped with his family before the Holocaust and leaving so many millions to be murdered, including his childhood sweetheart. Unable to face the past, he married a woman named Ruth as a surrogate for his childhood sweetheart, but he has also been unfaithful to her. At the same time that he is involved in his affair with Patricia, his imaginary self is in Germany trying to discover how little Ruth died and what happened to those who murdered her.

The destructive quality of Joel's love for Patricia underlies the split in his personality. Patricia, "a Christian in Jerusalem. . .in all its no man's lands," is merely a symbol of the temporal and spiritual disorientation that afflicts him. Joel's Holocaust has brought his problem to the surface, but it is not his real problem. Once little Ruth lost her leg in an accident, Joel no longer could love her the way he felt he should. Even though he transfers his love to another Ruth, sexual satisfaction and a clear conscience still elude him. When he takes the pains to discover what happened to little Ruth, he is distracted by his desire for the sexual relationship he needs and craves. Hence, his affair with Patricia represents what he could not have with little Ruth. Ruth, the religionist and Patricia, the devotee of Eros, both offer salvation. Ruth's salvation is through traditional religious faith and values, but Joel can no longer believe in these. Patricia's small breasts and childish manners make her a legitimate substitute for little Ruth, and her seductive legs intimate an erotic object that Ruth, who was crippled, cannot provide. In replacing little Ruth, Patricia supplies both Eros and Thanatos which attracts Joel; as a consequence, his sexual appetite overcomes his guilt. Since forgetfulness alone is not really atonement, Joel can only atone for his multiple infidelities with his death, itself the product of his self-indulgent desire to overcome his guilt.

Hanoch Bartov

In his novel *The Brigade*, Hanoch Bartov presents an alternate treatment of the issues raised by Amichai and Ben Amotz.[61] The hero, Elisha Kruk, through a conscious confrontation with the Holocaust experience that caused the deaths of relatives in his family and colored his own childhood memories, learns to perceive the world through adult eyes without compromising his own human worth. Unlike Joel in *Not of This Time, Not of This Place* and Uri in *To Remember, To Forget*, Elisha, an adolescent who was born in Palestine just learning to find his own direction in life, he carries buried within himself a hidden guilt that he associates with sexual impotence and that emerges in the form of self-pity. Having enlisted at the age of sixteen in the British Army, ostensibly to fight the Germans in order to escape what he considers to be the intellectually frustrating and socially stifling atmosphere of his home, he finds himself thrust into a world that epitomizes all those moral tensions and from which he plans to escape.

Throughout the novel, Elisha tries to behave like an adult by conforming to adult expectations, but he feels that he is a child when he fails to win acceptance by his peers or his sexual partners. When Elisha refuses Brodsky's invitation to a whorehouse, he pleads: "Don't want to. Don't need it. I'm a child." His refusal is linked with what he interprets as childish innocence; but as the novel develops, the reader observes and Elisha learns that it always results in decisions that are grounded in ethical judgments that require a great deal of maturity. Plagued by his "childish thoughts" he remembers Noga, his faithless teen-age sweetheart and her taunt, "You're a child Elisha. . .a child. . .child. . .child," and when he is ill at ease in the brothel where Pinik presents the whore, Felicia, she suggests, "let the poor boy eat something." It is the mature narrator who reflectively notes, "I later learned. . .a man's age is not only the total of his years."

At the beginning of the novel, Elisha is infected with "honey-coated altruism" and at the same time that he is plagued with guilt. When he fouls himself in a hospital, he feels dirty inside. His parents' pleas that he return home to help them also elicit pangs of guilt. He is plagued by sins he did not commit which in turn infect him with a "blubbering and sensitivity," a "bearing of the world's pain" on his shoulders. This guilt stems from the rejection of his past:

> At last I was as I had always wanted to be right where I'd wanted to be ever since I was smacked with a ruler in the *moshava's* Hebrew school when I was seven, ever since I got fed up with my *keppela* and *tzitzis* when I was ten, ever since I fled the factory and my home, fled the web of duty and boredom that held me bound in an invisible cage.

Having gone to a religious school and remembering with nostalgia the Sabbath traditions of his father's house, it is small wonder that Elisha's memories plague him in the absurd world of post-Holocaust Europe. When he confronts the refugees from the camps and meets a Krochmal who might be a relative, he sees himself as a man with a mission. He begins to identify more fully with Zunenshein, a sensitive man for whom life in postwar Germany is an unnerving experience. He rejects the crude cries for vengeance of the cantor at a memorial service, Giladi's impatience with Tamari's call for restraint in dealing with German women, and Brodsky's appeal that Elisha allow Jewish soldiers to rape the German women in whose houses they were quartered.

Elisha's maturation IS linked with his coming to accept that his intense but childish romance with Noga is over and that the easy sexual gratifications sought by Brodsky and his childhood idol, Pinik, cannot provide the satisfaction he seeks. At the beginning of the novel, Noga writes daily. During the war and Elisha's absence, the relationship cools, and Elisha finds that her letters end with the single word "yours." Realizing that the relationship was doomed from its inception, Elisha felt compelled to test it; with all his pompous self-pity, he failed to understand what Noga really loved in him:

"You can't fool me. You're very sensitive even it you are
a little neurotic. . . .I love you the way you are—an ugly
soul in a beautiful body."

The analysis of Noga's soul as ugly is accurate, for she rejects Elisha
in favor of Rivkin, a lawyer who will provide her with the comforts
that befit her station in Israeli society: "One thing's sure, you don't
have to worry about Noga Reznik. She's fixed for life. Well, you'll
see." The erotic infatuation that intoxicated Elisha in his childish
affair with Noga recurs when he is lost in the arms of Felicia. Swoon-
ing lustfully in Felicia's arms, he dreams of his long ago one-night
indiscretion with Noga. Although Elisha rejects Brodsky's call to a
prostitute out of fidelity to Noga, his disappointment with her
engagement to Rivkin draws him into the hands of a whore, only
to realize that she is a source of delusion rather than fulfillment.

Just as Felicia serves as Noga's erotic double whose felicity is
inherent in her name, Uncle Pinik embodies all that is nihilistic
and demonic in Elisha's adolescent experience. It was with Pinik
that Elisha first violated Jewish dietary practices. Pinik represents
the rejection of authority and restraint that Elisha desperately but
irresponsibly craves; Pinik admits that Elisha's father was "respect-
able to the end" and Elisha recalls his childhood musings: "When I
grow up, I used to tell myself, I'll be like Pinik. The exact opposite
of Father." While his enlistment in the British army is an expression of adolescent rebellion, Elisha's confrontation with Pinik
forces him to affirm those values that Pinik rejects. He poses the
rhetorical question, "Why on earth did you run off to the army?"
and adds the accusation, "You're just a kid." Like Pinik, the childish
Elisha runs from his problems; Pinik can never grow up into mature
adulthood because of his constant irresponsible indulgences. It is this
grotesque flight from responsibility that brings Elisha to notice
that he is taller, and by implication, more mature than his uncle.
Elisha's maturity first exhibits itself when he cannot understand
how Pinik could dance at a wedding when the civilized world is
collapsing around him because of Hitler's madness. Ultimately it
is through the restraint fostered by religion and the discipline of
his father, a man whom Pinik admits "never did anything forbidden," that Elisha learns to accept responsibility and achieve adulthood. Significantly, maturity brings Elisha to reject Pinik and his
nihilistic world view: ". . .(we do what is forbidden) because it is
forbidden. Otherwise we'd have no rules to break."

Elisha's final test comes when he refuses to listen to the appeal
of a fellow soldier, Brodsky, that he permit the Jewish soldiers to

rape the German women in whose houses they are quartered. His action is an expression of pure integrity; he wanted to be as humane to his enemy as he could. The sexually active, mature soldiers lack the ethical sensitivity that is adulthood. Once he withstands Brodsky and the nameless soldier whose crime he prevented, Elisha is able to combine the values of his childhood and adolescence with the strength of his manhood.[62] His enlistment in the British army force him to confront the nihilistic fantasies of his youth and to discover the balance of traditional Judaic values that make him into a man who must live with these values and knows he cannot compromise: "Thank God I did not destroy myself in Germany, thank God that was beyond me. I am what I am."

Chapter 4

The Holocaust as Redemptive Catalyst: Rebirth in Israel

Amos Oz

In *Touch the Water, Touch the Wind*, Amos Oz, who was born in Jerusalem in 1939, presents an interpretation of the search of the Jewish survivors of the Holocaust for meaning and salvation in the tradition of earlier works of Hebrew fiction.[63] Like Ka-Tzetnik in *Phoenix Over the Galilee* and Amichai in *Not of This Time, Not of This Place*, Oz has created a hero in search of redemption through means of dual points of view. Beginning his tale at the point where Elisha Pomeranz and his wife, Stefa, are separated and continuing the narrative in alternating narrative lines that eventually converge when husband and wife are finally reunited in Israel, Oz orchestrates that cosmic messianic dream hidden in the recesses of Pomeranz's mind. Elisha Pomeranz, like Harry Preleshnik, is a messianic figure paralleling the life of Jesus. Hiding in the Polish forest in the early winter of 1938, Elisha assumes the identity of a peasant woodcutter named Dziobak Przywolski, a man who claimed to be of virgin birth and who performed miracles of healing. He had been axed to death when he boasted that if he were smitten with an ax, the ax would break; this nonmiracle took place on Good Friday. Similarly, Elisha's name in Hebrew means "my God will save," the Hebrew name, *Yehoshua*, also means "God will save." It is this quest for salvation that permeates the novel, for Elisha often does and says things that are associated with the Christ of the Gentiles. On two occasions, Elisha would "render unto the Kibbutz that which belongs to the Kibbutz," echoing Jesus' admonition to render unto Caesar the things that are Caesar's and unto God the things that are God's.[64]

When in Israel, Elisha gravitates to Galilee, the region of Palestine where most of the ministry of Jesus centered.

If Oz's symbolic language invests Pomeranz with messianic qualities, the narrative portrays him as one who is able to float above the world as if he were God:

> He rose and floated on the dark air, his body slack after the effort borne high and silent over woods and meadows, over churches, huts and fields.
> So he overcame all the obstacles in his way.

The son of a watchmaker, Elisha examines the universe from a perspective that tries to make sense of an apparently meaningless cosmos. His cosmic outlook on the world appears on various occasions:

> Even material objects, if you plumb their depths, are no more than vague images. In brief: ideas cannot be perceived, and perceptible objects can never be grasped by thought.

Pomeranz believes his mission is to instill a "different inner rhythm" in "haunted souls," to gain "the power to work wonders, to reveal something of the harmony of the spheres, to work some kind of salvation."

His submission to his own physical wants, especially his momentary lapse with Audrey, is something that Pomeranz finds repulsive: "Prolonged celibacy: relations of pent-up boredom, of faint disgust, with the inescapable body, with its whims, its demands, its impositions." This opinion of the physical world is remarkably similar to that of the German philosopher Arthur Schopenhauer.[65] According to Schopenhauer, the physical world imposes upon man a physical form that limits his ability to transcend the world of the senses and intuit a world of pure will—the "thing-in-itself." It is through Pomeranz's metaphysical use of mathematics, logic, and music—the same vehicles through which Schopenhauer tactically contemplates the subjectivity of his own will and thereby could view his self as an object freed from limiting will—that Pomeranz seeks to engage in "mending" or (*tikkun*), correcting the world. His *mending* of watches is an allusion to the correction of subjective time, which according to Schopenhauer is likewise a necessary corrective to man's willful perception. By overcoming time, Pomeranz achieves a metaphysical understanding of the universe. Significantly, the first name of Professor Zaicek, who is Stefa's elderly intellectual mentor and the leader of the philosophical Goethe society and who is also the son of a watchmaker, is Emanuel, which alludes to the biblically mentioned son of the young woman who, according to Christian tradition, is the virgin who conceives the Redeemer.[66] When visitors come searching for Pomeranz to make him known to the world, alert man A said to alert man B: "He's set the whole world buzzing and now he's lost somewhere in this goddam silence." Alert man B responds: "As soon as you said silence, goddam silence, I could hear the sound of an animal, a barking perhaps, and there's a rhythmic throbbing noise on the other side of this hill."

The translation "goddam silence" is an unfortunate rendering of the Hebrew, *dumiyat Elohim*, or "Divine Silence."[67] Pomeranz is lost in a cosmic rhythm that is not so much damned, as the English version suggests, as it is blessed, and transcends human perception.

While Elisha is engaged in abstract metaphysical speculation throughout the novel, Stefa, who seems young and flighty at the novel's beginning, develops into a calculating and resourceful political tactician. Rather than accompany him into the forest, she has remained behind, unafraid of the Germans. A devotedly European-ized Jew, she feels her religious and racial ancestry to be incidental and her loyalties to the ideas of Martin Heidegger to be such that her universal idealism will preserve her.[68] The local intelligentsia could not understand how "such an intelligent, artistic young lady" could give "herself to the dreamy son of a simple watchmaker." Her enlightenment, or more precisely her disenchantment with European culture, and the dream of a cultural and political unification begin with the outbreak of active war, which, for "all its horrors and its vulgarity, had offered a certain possibility of rejuvenating Europe." As the novel progresses, she bitterly discovers that the rejuvenation is not to be. The migraine headaches from which she first began to suffer at the beginning continue until she arranges her defection from Russia. These migraines reflect and are indicative of her inability to accept the senseless brutal world that surrounds her. When the Poles and Germans skin a Russian bear and serve it to the guests at a banquet, Stefa suffers "a certain hardening." She is drawn to the son of the watchmaker whom she deserted before she realized that his skepticism was more justified than her optimism.

Stefa's hard new insights enable her to reach Moscow where she acquires a Russian husband. She also recalls with longing the son of the watchmaker when she is alone with Mikhail Andreitch, whom she uses to help her find the watchmaker's son whom she desires.

Throughout the novel, people look to Stefa for the satisfaction of the sexual lust that consumes them. Just as the intelligentsia at the Goethe Society disguise their interest in Stefa's legs with polite intellectual banter, the "ancient retired revolutionaries" are no more ideologically oriented than their Polish and German counterparts; they, too, exploit her body in the name of "the cause."

While Stefa and Elisha Pomeranz are separated through the course of the novel, they share a disgust for a singularly corrupt and inhuman world. Audrey, the nihilistic, immature vagabond, becomes the object of Elisha's sexual indiscretion. For Elisha, in his sleepy free associations, she is connected with the godless malevolent forces of the commercialized modern world. "Howling wolves. Vampires. Ax blow. Forests upon forests. Snow. Greek music. American banknotes. Audrey. . . simple elements and violent combinations."

This vulgar world is always associated with pork fat. The "nauseating Germans" disgust him to the point of physical pain: "Metaphysical wrong cannot be perceived, while perceptible wrong emits a powerful stench of pork fat."

The phrase "pork fat" is again used when Stefa is commanded to play the music of Schubert and Chopin at the banquet where the Russian bear was tried, skinned, and served to the guests. This unholy alliance of the Poles and Germans is, as the author comments, "a marriage of souls in melancholy splendor. . .pork cooked in pork fat." Pomeranz's four-day affair with Audrey liberates his body physically while it defiles him spiritually. The author, in describing Elisha's free associations, juxtaposes metaphysical perceptions with the "clumsy ephermeral convergence of abstract energies," and "pork fat" with the "potency of grace." The violent attack upon the kibbutz in Israel where Stefa and Elisha are finally reunited is dismissed as "merely clumsy and banal. . . saturated with pork fat." The many allusions to pork fat all symbolize the ugliness of human experience. While Stefa and Elisha Pomeranz are drawn together by their mutual rejection of the alien world of pork fat, those Jews who succumb to avaricious greed are said to be making a fortune in canned beef. Yotam, the son of Ernst, the secretary of the kibbutz, who having gotten into trouble has been sent to Argentina to mature, finds that he enjoys the luxury of Diaspora life in the canned-beef exporting business. After Mikhail Andreitch fails to keep Stefa from defecting, he seeks political asylum and eventually makes a fortune in canned beef.

The author's frequent allusions to pork fat and Jewish canned beef symbolize the degenerate culture of Western civilization. Irrespective of the political ideology that artifically legitimizes that baseness whether it be National Socialist, Communist, or, for that matter, Zionist, basic animal greed arises to debase and negate humanity's professed ideals. The Holocaust is but one manifestation of that continuing debasement; Stefa and Elisha Pomeranz never embrace any political ideology because they need no surrogate in their mutual quest for salvation.

Yitzhak Shenhar

No study of Hebrew literature would be complete if it did not include works that depict those Israelis who have been displaced or whose lives have been changed because of the Holocaust. Yitzhak Shenhar's "On Galilean Shores," and Yehuda Ya'ari's "Three-fold Palestine" affirm the roots the Jews in Germany were denied.

"On Galilean Shores" represents one of Shenhar's more hopeful treatments of a German Jew's return to the heritage of his fore-fathers.[69] The hero, Theo, takes his library with him when after having completed two semesters at a German university, his studies are terminated by the disintegrating political atmosphere in the Germany of his youth. While he steadily becomes more and more committed to his Jewish heritage, the women characters in "On Galilean Shores" are less than enthusiastic about Zionism and the national Jewish revival. Uri's assimilated sister mourns the "better days that are irrevocably gone," and she is concerned lest her son, Uri, "will forget the mother language." Geulah, the heroine, also vacillates between her traditional Zionist heritage and her longing to see the larger world and take part in what Shenhar depicts as the decadent middle-class society of Tel Aviv's night life.

Although the narrative line is clear, the symbolic language and its implications make "On Galilean Shores" a clever but sometimes confusing short story. For Shenhar, daylight represents the visible but ephermeral reality while night connotes the metaphysical con-tinuum of history and eternity.[70] Phenomenal vision in the daylight is in itself misleading; the true seer understands the meaning of the historical continuum and watches for it in the dark. Reb Jehiel

Michel Schwartz, Geulah's grandfather and one of the founders of the settlement, is such a person. A religious man, his place is in the synagogue, a building that seems to "need nothing but the vault of heaven above." His skullcap is reminiscent of the cloud that covers the top of Mount Hermon, thereby implying that he, like the mountain and the sky, is an integral part of the eternal Jewish experience in Palestine. He is awake at night and watchful when the sunlight no longer bothers him; his eyes have a "habit of screwing up during the daytime, but toward evening they are wide open and their deep sockets reveal traces of light blue." At night Reb Jehiel appreciates the unchanging constancy of what he perceives to be Israel's enduring mission.

This elderly pioneer finds in Theo an avid student. Before Theo speaks with Reb Jehiel, he "stands and looks, and the lenses of his glasses gleam in the sunlight." Unable to distinguish between the eternal and the temporal reality, the still assimilated Theo stands blinded in the daylight. After his encounter with Reb Jehiel, he learns to "squint with his weak eyes"; he becomes aware of the "night dampness which covers the ground." He then "stretches out on the grass and feels as though his being is absorbed by some great essence." Once committed to his serving as watchman or guardian of the Jewish fate, Theo realizes that "there is no room for levity in life." Conversely, the cynical Geulah "could not visualize anything clearly," dazzled as she is by the bright lights of Tel Aviv and the artificiality of the city's night life.

Only the watchmen in Shenhar's story are aware of the historical mission of Israel and only they understand the difference between the empirical sight of the present day and Israel's larger historical significance: "Vision and reality don't go together. Vision goes straight and reality in roundabout ways, they only have the same starting point." The reality perceived by the Israeli night watchmen is implicit in the names of the story's characters. Jehiel Michel Schwarts means "God is living," "who is like God," and "black." His given names ascribe praise to the Lord, and his surname refers to the nightlike eternity of his world outlook. The name Theo refers to God, but it is Greek in derivation, reflecting his assimilated origins. Reb Jehiel's granddaughter's name, Geulah, means "redemption." She joins Theo on her return to the village after her abortive venture into Tel Aviv society. They go together to listen to the songs from the kibbutz: "Theo and Geula stood in the darkness outside and gazed inside the window and listened; and the touch of their bare arms felt warm in the coolness of the night." When Theo and Geula sleep together at night, the forces implicit in their names—

"God" and "redemption"–converge in a redemptive union which confirms the belief and hope of Geula's grandfather, Reb Jehiel. Ironically, Geula needs Theo to affirm her own roots. Commitment to the land of Israel redeems both the assimilated Jew fleeing from what proved to be the central tragedy in modern Jewish history as well as the less-committed Zionist whose thirst for personal fulfillment sometimes outweighed her patriotism.

Yehuda Ya'ari's "Three-fold Palestine" is a story about the decision of an assimilated German Jew, Richard Oppenheimer, to circumcise his son.[71] At the story's conclusion, both the reader and narrator learn that Richard himself was never circumcised because his father did not want his son to be burdened by the sign of the Abrahamic covenant in anti-Semetic German society. Unlike his father, Richard willingly accepts for his son what his assimilationist father sought to deny. By involving his father in the circumcision of his son, Richard is in effect enlisting himself, and his father, as well as his son, in the fold of Israel.

Richard's commitment is not really appreciated by the narrator, whose superficial Zionism is both smug and complacent. Annoyed that Richard answers his good morning with the German *guten morgen* instead of the Hebrew *boker tov*, he finds it distastefully amusing that Richard does not know a word of Hebrew when he is asked to help Richard recite the circumcision blessing for his son. The narrator sees the profile of Esau in the Germanic Richard, intimating that Richard projects a Gentile countenance.[72] Ya'ari is comparing the simplistic and shallow perspective of the self-righteous Zionist with the sincere desire of a German Jew to reaffirm his ties with Jewry. Like Shenhar, Ya'ari views the Holocaust as a challenge to the postwar Jewish community. There is much salvaged; but only true commitment and affirmation can bring about the ingathering of those exiled.

Haym Hazaz

"Harat Olam," or "Creation of the World" is Haym Hazaz's most direct and scathing treatment of those assimilated Jews whom he believes have lost their ties with main-stream Jewry.[73] Undaunted by the betrayal of humanism and European liberalism, these immigrants to Palestine remain closer to the anti-Semitic society of their origins than they do to the new Israeli society. Like Hazaz's other stories, "Drabkin," "ha-Derashah," "Shelulit ha-Genuzah," and "Havit Achurah,"[74] "Harat Olam" reflects "the rise of Hitlerism and the Holocaust, both of which replaced the revolution in Hazaz's mind as evidence of the continual harsh trauma of Jewish experience."[75] Similarly, Hazaz's novel of the Russian revolution, *Gates of Bronze*, shows the many forces in Jewish cultural life to which his various characters are subject.[76] Tragically, these characters are stronger than their communal ties. But in the stories mentioned above, Hazaz is still preoccupied with the possibility of Jewry's physical and spiritual renewal. Although Hazaz finds a messianic spark in many of his characters, he is concerned with the need for vision or the talent to activate that spark.

In "Harat Olam," Hazaz presents an assimilated German Jew, Max Hershfield, whose mission in life is to transplant his middle-class life style into Israel while Moroshkeh, a committed Zionist, vainly tries to convince Max of the legitimacy of the Zionist cause. Max is unimpressed with all the arguments and erudition that Moroshkeh can muster, but when he finds that Moroshkeh has a nodding acquaintance with Plato, he becomes respectful. Only when Moroshkeh shows that he can transcend what, from Max's perspective, are

111

parochial Jewish attitudes can Max appreciate his remarks. For
Hazaz, the Holocaust is but one of many recurring catastrophies
that the Jewish people have suffered. Unlike the romantic Ya'ari or
the cautiously hopeful Shenhar, Hazaz views the Holocaust not as a
deviation in history but as the norm. While ethnic salvation is possible, Hazaz is cautiously noncommitted concerning the possibility
of its being brought to fruition.

S.Y. Agnon

Hebrew fiction's Nobel Laureate, S.Y. Agnon, did not write about the Holocaust in an explicit way. Still, he was very concerned about the integration of assimilated German Jews into Israeli society, as well as finding a response to the Holocaust. *A Guest for the Night*, his major novel, written in 1939 just before the outbreak of World War II, may well anticipate the imminent disintegration of European Jewry that resulted from the Holocaust. According to Arnold Band, "While it is impossible to attribute to Agnon prophetic foreknowledge of the Holocaust of World War II, one cannot neglect the *Sitz im Leben* of "Oreah Notel La-Lun.""[77]

Similarly, Gershon Shaked has stated that *A Guest for the Night* articulates the "human condition" between the two World Wars and the Holocaust.[78] Since Agnon never deals with the Holocaust directly, the critic can only reconstruct his attitude toward it on the basis of themes and motifs that recur throughout his fiction.

Like Shenhar, Hazaz, Ya'ari, Amichai, and Ben Amotz, Agnon shares the stereotypic biases concerning the assimilated German Jew who feels closer to an anti-Semitic German host culture than to the Jewish community in Palestine. Many of his stories deal with the psychological makeup of such people. In *Sippur Pashut*, he describes the frustrated love of Hershel, who, because of his own lack of initiative and his inability to overcome the wishes of his overbearing mother, marries Minna Tzimlich rather than Beluma Nacht, his enchanting true love. Beluma's beauty, charm, and grace are antithetical to Hershel's superficial middle-class mediocrity. Unable to reconcile his misplaced love with his marital frustration, Hershel, in an act of self-affirmation, goes mad. His madness is an act of courage because he thereby transcends the shallowness and complacency that his culture has imposed upon him. Once cured, Hershel learns to suppress his unhappiness by ignoring the source of his insanity. He is not cured; he has only learned to accept his limitations.

Agnon's posthumous novel, *Shirah*, deals with themes not unlike those of *Sippur Pashut*. Written between the years 1948 and 1953, the book centers around a sexually frustrated scholar who is dissatisfied with middle-class Hebrew University life, but is unable to find a woman who can redeem him from his uncreative torpor.[79] German scholars like Manfred Herbst are as a rule more interested in secular than religious studies. Secularism by its very nature cannot provide the ultimate answers he seeks, and his work is therefore unsatisfying. A Jew devoid of religious education or values, Herbst would like to have an adulterous relationship with Shirah, the woman whom he believes can redeem him from his mediocrity and boredom. But like Hershel in *Sippur Pashut*, he can find no underlying unity in the mundane works of his life or in the disorganized results of his research.

Although Agnon's attitude toward Jacob Rechnitz in the tale "Betrothed" is more positive, the traditional stereotypes remain.[80] A marine biologist, Rechnitz is a committed scholar who studies the algae off the coast of Palestine. Like Herbst who studies Byzantine history, Rechnitz does not deal with Jewish matters directly because he considers himself a man of science.

While Rechnitz believes that he is an objective and logical student of nature, he is oblivious of the mythological and personal forces that surge within him. Each of the six girl friends, who revolve around him like planets, want to marry him, but he has promised to marry Susan Ehrlich, the daughter of a German consul who was once Jacob's patron. When it seems as though Jacob may well break his vow, Susan falls into a deep sleep. Miraculously she awakens and reappears to claim him from the six girl friends by winning the race they have arranged to determine who is to marry him. By winning, Susan becomes "Shoshanat Ya'akov" (the rose of Jacob). Like the traditional Hebrew expression associated with the Purim liturgy, they belong together; redemption, even in a secular setting, is dependent upon the proper union of the people who belong together.

"Edo ve-Enam" is one of Agnon's most enigmatic tales. The story revolves around an "objective" German professor, Dr. Ginat, who competes with Gamzu for the attention of Gemulah, Gamzu's wife.[81] A traditional scholar and romantic, Gamzu never approaches Gemulah, a woman from an old tribe with ancient traditions and an archaic language. Ginat, a detached critical investigator, draws Gemulah to him so that he can learn about her past and her people. Gemulah is attracted by the modern but sterile Ginat, who views her as an object of scholarship, while she disdains her husband whose medieval orientation bores her. Significantly, Gamzu never consummates his marriage with Gemulah. Ginat is, tragically, too dispassionate to become involved with her emotionally; he even tells her to return to her husband.[82] Like Susan in "Betrothed," Gemulah sleepwalks when she feels betrayed. Since Ginat is as impotent as Gamzu in his relationship with her, albeit for different reasons, she carries Ginat and herself to their deaths in a final act of sleepwalking. Ironically, Ginat's attempt to rescue Gemular represents the one altruistic act he performs in the course of the story; once he becomes involved with Gemulah, he, like Gamzu, cannot satisfy her.[83]

Just as Agnon's German characters are modern individuals for whom traditional values and restraints are either unknown or irrelevant, his novel *A Guest for the Night*, depicts the disintegration of European Jewry and its values on the eve of the Holocaust.[84] For Agnon, the German Jew is a victim of the modern European world's spiritual rape of traditional values; in *A Guest for the Night* he presents the dying gasp of traditional Jewish society before a thoroughly demonic modern secularism eradicates it entirely. While the German Jew cannot perceive the approaching Holocaust, the traditional Jew, aware of the differences between his private world based on ancient tradition and an antagonistic modern secularism, is unable to prevent the approaching catastrophe. In *A Guest for the Night*, the narrator is a traditional Jew whom modernity has already corrupted with the cynicism of doubt. He returns to Shibush (which means corruption), his ancestral town, before the Day of Atonement. Hoping to be cleansed of his modern malaise, he finds the traditional world of his childhood to be in decline. In his discussion with Pinhas Aryeh, an ultra-Orthodox politician, he states:

> I do not say that we, as opposed to you, live by the Torah, but we want to live by it—only the vessels of our souls are broken, and cannot hold it.

Alluding to the Kabbalistic doctrine of the "broken vessels," the narrator confesses that he would like to believe in a complete and convincing religion, but modernity cannot sustain wholehearted beliefs.[85] To his disappointment, the narrator learns that his ancestral world will not offer him the models or the inspiration he seeks because it, too, has been corrupted.

Shibush represents a traditional Judaism in decline, its spiritual blight paralleled by the physical and spiritual blemishes of its inhabitants. The city's *bet midrash*, or study house, is now empty; only the guest has the luxury of keeping it open because he alone has the artificial luxury of studying the Torah. In light of his confession to Pinhas Aryeh, the narrator's study of the Torah is nostalgic and not an activity that reflects real interests and pursuits. Yeruham Hofshi and Daniel Bloch rebel against a religious tradition whose God is either silent or impotent. Ignatz and Rubberovich are physically deformed, and Reb Hayim's early promise as a rabbinic scholar is wasted and ends tragically in a broken marriage. The narrator's journey to the world of his youth, like those of Uri in *To Remember, To Forget*, and of Joel in *Not of This Time, Not of This Place*, is an attempt to find atonement for some blemish he feels but cannot articulate. For Agnon, Palestine provides the redemptive tonic for post-Holocaust Jewry; in *A Guest for the Night*, only those characters who immigrate to Palestine find satisfaction and happiness. When he finds that he has taken the key to the *bet midrash* of Shibush to Palestine, he is transporting what is salvageable to the modern new reality of Israel.

Overview

The striking consistency in all the works of Israeli literature bearing on the Holocaust and the destruction of the European Jewish people is their concern for the redemptive possibilities of the aftermath. The Nazi scourge represents a world in which all moral imperatives were null and void. By affirming their love of their own culture and their faith in themselves, post-Holocaust Israeli writers attempt to make sense of their situation, even though the tragic enormity of the Holocaust defies explanation.[86]

Despite their many artistic, ideological, and political differences, Hebrew writers on the theme of the Holocaust share a common concern for the possibility of reconciliation and redemption in the post-Holocaust world. All of Ka-Tzetnik's protagonists yearn for salvation. Moni and Daniella are "liberated" from the Nazis by death, but Harry's physical emancipation leaves him unredeemed until he learns to love Galilea. The very title of Yoram Kaniuk's *Adam Resurrected* hints at its chronicle of one who must rise from death to find life of a post-Holocaust sanity. In "My Little Sister," Abba Kovner presents a futile search for redemption on the part of brothers who died in the Holocaust, but whose sister was "saved" in a convent. Uri Tzvi Greenberg's poetry possesses as eschatological quality that finds in the Holocaust tragedy the possibility of national revival. It is unfortunate that much of his poetry is not yet available to the English reading public.

T. Carmi's René and Ben Amotz's Uri Lam both learn to accept their lot as Holocaust survivors; René is an orphan, and Uri comes to recognize that he cannot escape the past but has the right to survive. Max, in Appelfeld's "Bertha" and Joel, in Amichai's *Not of This Time, Not of This Place*, both exploit women to heal their psychological wounds. Neither Max nor Joel recognize that Bertha's warmth or Patricia's sexuality cannot solve his emotional problems. In Bartov's *The Brigade* and Oz's *Touch the Wind, Touch the Water*, the protagonist's first name is Elisha, which means "God will save." Elish Kruk in *The Brigade* is saved by the affirmation of his childhood values in an amoral adult world, and Elisha of *Touch the Wind, Touch the Water* is obviously a messianic figure who parallels Jesus.[86]

Shenhar, Yizhar, Agnon, and Hazaz all reflect the hope for redemption, not only in their Holocaust writings, but in their other works as well. The modern Hebrew writer is more secular than his ancestors, but nevertheless, his works embody the traditional Jewish response to the suffering of Israel and the hope for future salvation.

Notes

1. According to Northrup Frye, the recurring use of archetypes creates a literary mythology that is "an abstract of a purely literary world of fictional and thematic design, unaffected by canons of plausible adaptation to familiar experience. In terms of narrative, myth is the imitation of actions near or at the conceivable limits of desire. . . .The world of mythical imagery is usually represented by the concept of heaven or Paradise in religion, and it is apocalyptic in the sense that the world is already explained, a world of total metaphor, in which everything is potentially identical with everything else" (*Anatomy of Criticism*, Princeton: Princeton University Press, 1957, p. 136). Literary myth contains the world view that underlies and unifies the creator's grasp of the universe. While the critic does not *evaluate* the worth of any given work on the basis of the ideas it contains, the literary historian examines the consistency of themes and ideas that occur in the literature of a particular period or genre.

2. Percy Lubbock in *The Craft of Fiction* (New York: Viking, 1973, p. 12) argues that the critic should only be concerned with the aesthetic analysis of the novel. Authorial intention, imagination, choice of subject matter, are not really elements of "the craft of fiction." Similarly authorial ideology, or authorial world view, is not the concern of the literary critic. The ideational or intellectual dimension is not inherently relevant to the aesthetic worth of a work; it is only the integration of ideas into the artistic structure that should be considered by the literary critic. According to Welleck and Warren, "the close integration between philosophy and literature is frequently deceptive, and the arguments in its favor are overrated because they are based on a study of literary ideology, professions of intentions, and programmes which, necessarily borrowing from aesthetic formulations, may sustain only remote relationship to the actual practice of the artists" (*Theory of Literature*, New York: Harcourt, Brace, & World, 1956, p. 121).

3. Ka-Tzetnik 135633 is the pen name of Karol Cetynski. A "Ka-Tzet" is a concentration camp; a Ka-Tzetnik is a concentration camp inmate.

4. Quoted from the book jacket of *Atrocity* (New York: Lyle Stuart, 1963). The original edition in Hebrew is *Qareu Lo Peipel* (Tel Aviv: Am Oved, 1961).

5. Ibid.

6. Quoted from the book jacket of *Phoenix Over the Galilee* (New York: Harper & Row, 1969). The original Hebrew edition is *Ke-Hol Me-Afar* (Tel Aviv: Am Oved, 1966).

7. Ka-Tzetnik 135633. *Atrocity* (New York: Lyle Stuart, 1963); *House of Dolls* (New York: Simon & Schuster, 1955) originally published in Yiddish under the title *Dos Hoyz fun di Lalkes* (Tel Aviv: Peretz, 1952). *Phoenix Over the Galilee* (New York: Harper & Row, 1969). All quotations from these novels in the text were taken from these editions.

8. The device of beginning the narration in *media res*—in the middle of the action—was first used by the Greek classical dramatists. By employing this technique, Ka-Tzetnik presents his own versions of modern tragedy complete with a malevolent setting and protagonists whose tragic flaw is their innocence and naiveté. (See Beckson and Ganz, *A Reader's Guide to Literary Terms* (New York: Farrar, Straus, and Giroux, 1960, pp. 51-52).

9. Daniella and Moni are unaware of the implications of their hideous predicaments until they realize that their destruction is inevitable. Their subjective outlook tells more about their own characters than it does about the situations they describe at Auschwitz. Ka-Tzetnik uses their brother, Harry, as a factually reliable observer who articulates a position similar to the author's. For an authoritative study of point of view and narrative technique, see Wayne C. Booth, *Rhetoric of Fiction* (Chicago: University of Chicago Press, 1973).

10. The English text reads, "On *Rosh Hashanah* their destiny is inscribed, and on *Yom Kippur* it is sealed, how many shall pass away and how many shall be brought into existence; who shall live and who shall die; who shall come to a timely end, and who to an untimely end; who shall perish by fire and who by water, who by sword and who by beast; who by hunger and who by thirst; who by earthquake and who by plague; who by strangling and who by stoning; who shall be at ease and who shall wander about" (Philip Birnbaum, trans., *High Holyday Prayer Book*, New York: Hebrew Publishing Company, 1951, p. 362).

11. The phoenix is a mythical Arabian bird that is said to live for five hundred years, after which it burns to death, only to spring reborn from its ashes. It thus represents an eternal cycle of being that transcends the conventional cycle of life and death.

12. Job 29:18. This translation, which is by Nina De-Nur, is the epigraph of *Phoenix Over the Galilee*.

13. Num. 35:21.

14. 1 Sam. 16:12.

15. See T.B. *Ketubot* 62b-63a and T.B. *Nedarim* 50a for the Talmudic account of Rachel's relationship with the plebian Aqiba. After having married Aqiba against her father's wishes, she sent him away to study.

16. See Zach. 9:9 and Matt. 21:5.

17. Yoram Kaniuk, *Adam Resurrected*, trans. Seymour Simckes (New York: Atheneum, 1971). All quotations from this novel in the text were taken from this edition. The original edition in Hebrew is *Adam ben Kelev* (Tel Aviv: Tel Aviv Publishers, 1969).

18. The full name of the institution is "Mrs. Seizling's Institute for Rehabilitation and Therapy."

19. The biblical source of this tradition is Esther 8:17.

20. See *Adon Olam* prayer in Joseph Hertz, *Daily Prayer Book* (New York: Bloch, 1959, p. 9): "He was, He is, He shall remain in glorious eternity."

KOVNER

21. Abba Kovner, "My Little Sister," in *A Canopy in the Desert*, trans. Shirley Kaufman (Pittsburgh: University of Pittsburgh Press, 1972). All the quotations in the text from this poem were taken from this work.

22. Ps. 24:4.

23. In the Sermon on the Mount, Jesus teaches that the poor, the sorrowful, the hungry, and the meek are fortunate or blessed (Matt. 5:2-10). Unlike Jesus, the little sister is not "thus crucified." Her passion and suffering continue until her death. Echoing Jesus, Kovner is really presenting a critque of a Christendom that continues to crucify the Jews:

> Blessed are ye, when men shall revile you, and persecute you, and shall say all manner of evil against you falsely, for my sake. Rejoice. . .for so persecuted they the prophets which were before you, (Matt 5:11 12).

The nine Dominican nuns are entirely unaware that the little Jewish girl is closer to the Lord than they are. Noting the extreme happiness that the idolized figure must be enjoying because of the adoration lavished on it by the nuns, the little sister, herself "crucified" by history, takes his place as the unredeemed sacrifice on the altar of time and history.

24. Deut. 23:19.

25. Song of Sol. 1:4.

26. *Op. cit.*

27. Isa. 28:1.

28. This formula is used when the groom bestows a ring upon his bride in fulfillment of the requirement that a woman must be betrothed by being endowed with money or its equivalent. See *Mishnah Kiddushin* 1:1 and *Shulhan Aruch-Even ha-Ezer* 27-1-2.

29. See 2 Sam. 1:23. The translated Hebrew text reads, "May the father of mercies, who dwelleth on high, in his mighty compassion, remember those

loving, upright, and blameless ones. . .who laid down their lives for the sanctifi-
cation of the divine Name, who were lovely and pleasant in their lives, and in
their death they were not divided; swifter than eagles, stronger than lions to do
the will of their master." Hertz, *Daily Prayer Book*, pp. 511-513.
30.   One cannot receive comfort from those who are alive. See Gen. 37:35 and
Rashi, *ad. loc.*

GREENBERG

31.   Baruch Kurzweil, *Ben Hazon le-Ven ha-Absurdi* (Jerusalem: Schocken,
1966, p. iii).
32.   See Ezra Spicehandler, "Greenberg, Uri Zvi," *Encyclopedia Judaica*
(Jerusalem: Keter, 1971, vol. 7).
33.   Uri Tzvi Greenberg, *Rehovot Hanahar* (Jerusalem: Schocken, 1968).
34.   Ruth Finer Mintz, ed. & trans., *Modern Hebrew Poetry* (Berkeley and
Los Angeles: University of California Press, 1968). All quotations from these
two poems in the text were taken from this edition.
35.   Kurzweil, op. cit., p. 50.

ALTERMAN

36.   Nimrod, who lived in Ur of the Chaldess, was a mighty hunter before the
Lord (Gen. 10:9), and rabbinic tradition has connected this ancient figure with
the child Abram. When Abram refused to worship the pagan god of fire, Nimrod
then condemned Abram to be cast into the fire (Hebrew, *ur*), and was saved by
the Lord. The source for this etiological legend is *Bereshit Rabbah* 38 and in a
slightly variant form, *Tana de-ve-Eliyahu* 6.
37.   The Hebrew version, "*Mikkol ha-Ammin*," can be found in Natan Gross,
ed., *Ha-Shoah be-Shirah ha-Ivrit* (Jerusalem: Yad Va-Shem & Kibbutz ha-
Meuhad, 1947, pp. 146-147). A partial translation may be found in Simon
Halkin, *Modern Hebrew Literature: Trends and Values* (New York: Schocken,
1970, pp. 137-138). All the quotations from this poem in the text were taken
from this work.
38.   See Hertz, *Daily Prayer Book*, pp. 799-801; the passage is taken from the
liturgy. It is on the Festivals when the Israelite is required to worship the Lord
in Jerusalem, and by so doing bear witness that he, as an Israelite, is a member
of the chosen people.
39.   See Lev. 3:2.

PAGIS

40. The English translation is from Dan Pagis, *Poems by Dan Pagis*, trans., Stephen Mitchell (Salisbury: Compton Press, 1972, p. 24). All the quotations in the text from these poems were taken from this work. The original poem in Hebrew can be found in Gross, op. cit., pp. 220-222.

41. Gen. 1:26.

42. Ibid., 3-19.

43. See Maimonides, *Sefer ha-Mada: Hilhot Yesodei ha-Torah* 1:9.

44. Pagis, op. cit., p. 32.

45. *Hevel* has this meaning in Eccles. 1:2. See also Robert Gordis, *Koheleth— The Man and His World* (New York: Jewish Theological Seminary of America, 1951, pp. 194-195).

CARMI

46. Mintz, *Modern Hebrew Poetry*, p. 324. All the quotations in the text of the poems are taken from this work.

47. The Hebrew term means "not mother," indicating that the head of the orphanage is not the little boy's biological mother.

48. René has no conception of the frailty of physical life or the finality of death. Just as the prophet Elijah was alive when he ascended to heaven in a chariot of fire, without dying, René envisions that his parents, rising to heaven on the smoke billowing up from the crematorium chimneys, are alive. See 2 Kings 2:11 and Mal. 3:23 for the biblical sources concerning Elijah's ascension.

49. Hos. 1:9 and 2:1.

APPELFELD

50. Leon I. Yudkin, *Escape into Siege: A Survey of Israeli Literature Today* (London: Routledge & Kegan Paul, 1974, p. 120).

51. S. Kremmer, *Realism u-Shevirato* (Tel Aviv, 1968), cited in Yudkin, op. cit.

52. The Hebrew version of this story was published by Aharon Appelfeld in *Ashan* (Jerusalem: Defus Yehudah, 1962). The English translation cited here is by T. Zindbank in S.Y. Penueli and A. Ukhmani, eds. *Hebrew Short Stories* (Tel Aviv: Megiddo, 1965). All the quotations in the text from this story were taken from this work. In an oral communication, Professor David Roskies of the Jewish Theological Seminary observed that Bertha's faithful knitting while Max is away provides an ironic twist to Penelope's weaving in the *Odyssey*.

GOURI

53.   Haim Gouri, *The Chocolate Deal*, trans. Seymour Simckes, (New York: Holt, Rinehart, & Winston, 1968). All quotations in the text from this novel were taken from this edition. The original Hebrew edition is *Iskat ha-Shokolat* (Tel Aviv: Kibbutz ha-Meuhad, 1965).
54.   Robert Alter, *After the Tradition: Essays on Modern Jewish Writing* (New York: Dutton, 1969, p. 171).

BEN AMOTZ

55.   Dahn Ben Amotz, *To Remember, To Forget*, trans. Eva Shapiro (Philadelphia: Jewish Publication Society of America, 1968). All the quotations in the text from this novel were taken from this edition.
56.   Yudkin, *Escape Into Siege*, p. 132. Yudkin fails to explain the thematic consequences of Uri's marriage to Barbara.
57.   It is interesting to note that Barbara accepts Uri's Judaism with greater ease than Uri accepts her Christianity. Like the biblical Ruth, the first "convert" to the religion of Israel, Barbara tells Uri that "wherever you go. . . .I will go."

AMICHAI

58.   Yehudah Amichai, *Not of This Time, Not of This Place*, trans. Shlomo Katz (New York: Harper & Row, 1963). All quotations in the text from this novel were taken from this edition. The original Hebrew edition is *Lo Me-Ahshaw, Lo Mi-Kan* (Tel Aviv: Schocken, 1963).
59.   Yudkin, *Escape Into Siege*, p. 131.
60.   See Max Arzt, *Justice and Mercy: Commentary on the Liturgy of the New Year and the Day of Atonement* (New York: Holt, Rinehart, & Winston, 1963, p. 119).

BARTOV

61.   Hanoch Bartov, *The Brigade*, Trans. David Segal (Philadelphia: Jewish Publication Society, 1967). All quotations in the text from this novel were taken from this edition. The original Hebrew edition is *Pitsei Bagrut* (Tel Aviv: Am Oved, 1965).
62.   While Alter admits that Elisha is consistently human, he argues that his behavior derives from weakness and indecision rather than moral strength. See Alter, *After the Tradition*, p. 178.

63. Amos Oz, *Touch the Water, Touch the Wind*, trans. Nicholas de Lange (New York: Harcourt, Brace, Jovanovich, 1973). All quotations in the text from this novel were taken from this edition. The original Hebrew edition is *La-Ga'at ba-Mayyim, La-Ga'at ba-Rush* (Tel Aviv: Am Oved, 1973).
64. See Matt. 22:21.
65. See Arthur Schopenhauer, *The World as Will and Idea*, trans. Haldene and Kemp (New York: Doubleday, 1961).
66. See Isa. 7:14 and Matt. 1:23.
67. See the Hebrew text, pp. 89-90.
68. Aside from Schopenhauer, which is the name of one of Stefa's cats, the only philosopher mentioned in the novel is Martin Heidegger, the German existentialist whose theory of being was exploited by the Third Reich. The distortion of pure ideas ultimately disappoints Stefa.

SHENHAR

69. Yitzak Shenhar, "On Galilean Shores," trans. Israel Schen in James Michener, *Firstfruits* (Philadelphia: Jewish Publication Society, 1973). All the quotations in the text from Shenhar's story were taken from this work.
70. This reading follows the approach of Professor Milton Arfa of New York University.
71. Yehuda Ya'ari, "The Three-fold Covenant," in *Jewish Heritage* (Fall 1964, pp. 59-63). Reprinted in *The Covenant*, ed. Isaac Halevy Levin (Jerusalem: Zionist Organization, 1965).
72. In Jewish literature, Esau represents the archetypal enemy of Israel.

HAZAZ

73. Haim Hazaz, *Seething Stones* [Hebrew]. (Tel Aviv: Am Oved, 1970).
74. The English translations of these titles are "The Sermon," "The Hidden Puddle," and "The Ugly Barrel."
75. Warren Bargad, *Character, Idea and Myth in the Works of Haim Hazaz* (Ann Arbor: University Microfilms, 1971, p. 159).
76. Haim Hazaz, *Gates of Bronze*, trans. Gerson Levi (Philadelphia: Jewish Publication Society, 1975). Although *Gates of Bronze* is not a Holocaust novel, it nevertheless reflects Hazaz's view of history which is an essential component of those works written during or about the Holocaust.

AGNON

77. Arnold Band, *Nostalgia and Nightmare* (Berkeley and Los Angeles: University of California Press, 1968, p. 285).
78. Gershon Shaked, *Omanut ha-Sippur shel Agnon* (Tel Aviv: Kibbutz ha-Artzi, 1973, p. 229). Concurring with Shaked are Harold Fisch, *S.Y. Agnon* (New York: Unger, 1975, p. 45), and Robert Alter, *After the Tradition*, p. 167.
79. Band, op. cit., p. 488.
80. The Hebrew title is *"Shevuat Emunim"* in *Ad Henah* (Jerusalem: Schocken, 1952). The English translation is by Walter Lever in S.Y. Agnon, *Two Tales* (New York: Schocken, 1966).
81. *"Edo ve-Enam"* was published in *Ad Henah* and in *Two Tales*.
82. See also Baruch Hochman, *The Fiction of S.Y. Agnon* (Ithaca: Cornell University Press, 1970, p. 6).
83. The name Ginat may be an oblique reference to Song of Solomon 6:11, where the beloved goes to the garden in hope of discovering if the fruits have ripened. Agnon's Ginat is objective to the point of sterility and cannot sustain a love relationship. This reading concurs with that of Fisch, pp. 38-39.
84. S.Y. Agnon, *A Guest for the Night*, trans. Misha Louvish (New York: Schocken, 1968). All quotations in the text from this novel were taken from this edition. The original Hebrew edition is *Oreah Noteh la-Lun* (Jerusalem: Schocken, 1967).
85. See Gershom Scholem, *Major Trends in Jewish Mysticism* (New York: Schocken, 1965, pp. 265-268).

OVERVIEW

86. Robert Alter arrives at a similar but not identical conclusion: "The writers do not seek to scare themselves or their readers with their stories, but, recognizing the necessity to exist now in the presence of the ultimate horror, they want to see by its baleful light what a Jew can discover about himself." See *After the Tradition*, p. 179.
87. 2 Kings 12-15. See also note 48.

Selected Bibliography

PRIMARY SOURCES: PROSE

Agnon, S.Y. *A Guest for the Night*. New York: Schocken, 1968.

――――. "Forevermore," Joel Blocker, ed. *Israeli Stories*. New York: Herzel, 1962, pp. 232-256.

――――. *Two Tales: Betrothed and Edo and Enam*. New York: Schocken, 1966.

Amichai, Yehuda. *Not of This Time, Not of This Place*. New York: Harper and Row, 1968.

――――. "My Father's Deaths." *Jewish Frontier* (October, 1960).

Appelfeld, Aharon. "Bertha." Penueli and Ukhmani, eds. *Hebrew Short Stories*. Tel Aviv: Megiddo, 1965.

――――. *In the Wilderness*. Jersualem: Ahshaw, 1965.

Bartov, Hanoch. *The Brigade*. Philadelphia: Jewish Publication Society, 1965.

Ben Amotz, Dahn. *To Remember, To Forget*. Philadelphia: Jewish Publication Society, 1968.

Dayan, Yael. *Death Has Two Sons*. New York: McGraw-Hill, 1968.

Gouri, Haim. *The Chocolate Deal*. New York: Holt, Rinehart & Winston, 1968.

Kaniuk, Yoram. *Adam Resurrected*. New York: Atheneum, 1971.

Ka-Tzetnik 135633. (Karol Cetynski). *Atrocity*. New York: Lyle Stuart, 1963.

――――. *House of Dolls*. New York: Simon & Schuster, 1955.

――――. *Phoenix Over the Galilee*. New York: Harper and Row, 1969.

――――. "Planet Auschwitz." *Jewish Digest* (April 1963).

Megged, Aharon, "The Name." Joel Blocker, ed. *Israeli Stories*. New York: Schocken, 1971, pp. 87-106.

Neshamit, Sarah. *The Children of Mapu Street*. Philadelphia: Jewish Publication Society, 1970.

Oz, Amos. *Touch the Water, Touch the Wind*. New York: Harcourt, Brace, Jovanovich, 1973.

Shenhar, Yitzhak. "On Galilean Shores." James Michener, ed. *Firstfruits*. Philadelphia: Jewish Publication Society, 1970.

Shilansky, Dov. *Mussulman*. Tel Aviv: Menora, 1962.

Shofman, Gershon. "The Two Old Men." *Palestine Tribune* (February 8, 1945) p. 4.

PRIMARY SOURCES: POETRY

Alterman, Natan. "And if need be,–Alone!" *Jewish Frontier* (March 1946), p. 43.

———. "From All Peoples," Simon Halkin, ed. *Modern Hebrew Literature*. New York: Schocken, 1970, pp. 137-138.

———. "The Dialogue between Nachshon and Gonen," M. Louvish, ed., *Flag of Freedom*. Jerusalem: Jewish National Fund., 1965, pp. 86-88.

———. "The Million." *Jewish Spectator* (May 1950).

———. "Mother, Now can I cry," Dov Vardi, ed. *New Hebrew Poetry*. Tel Aviv: WIZO, 1947, pp. 106-107.

———. "Prayer for Revenge," Dov Vardi, ed. *New Hebrew Poetry*. Tel Aviv: WIZO, 1947, pp. 166-167.

Amichai, Yehuda. "My Father." Burnshaw, et. al., eds. *The Modern Hebrew Poem Itself*. New York: Holt, Rinehart, and Winston, 1965, pp. 166-167.

———. "My Parent's Migrations." *Poems*. New York: Harper and Row, 1970, pp. 28-29.

Bavli, Hillel. "The Letter of the Ninety-three Maidens." *Reconstructionist* (March 5, 1943), p. 23.

Carmi, T. "Marcel's Song." *Jewish Quarterly* (Autumn 1960), p. 18.

———. "René's Songs." Ruth Finer Mintz, ed. and trans. *Modern Hebrew Poetry*. Berkeley and Los Angeles: University of California Press, 1968, pp. 328-338.

Efrat (Efros), Israel. "It Might Well Be." H.H. Fein, *Chapters in Modern Hebrew Literature*. New York: Hadassah, 1947, pp. 65-66.

Greenberg, Uri Tzvi. "Lord, You Saved Me From Ur-Germany as I Fled." Ruth Finer Mintz, ed. *Modern Hebrew Poetry*. Berkeley and Los Angeles: University of California Press, 1968, pp. 125-126.

———. "To God in Europe." Penueli and Ukhmani, eds. *Anthology of Modern Hebrew Poetry*. Jerusalem: Israel Universities Press, 1966, pp. 264-278.

———. "To the Mound of Corpses in the Snow." pp. 259-261.

———. "We Were Not Likened to the Dogs Among the Gentiles." Ruth Finer Mintz, ed. *Modern Hebrew Poetry*. Berkeley and Los Angeles: University of California Press, 1968, pp. 126-218.

———. "Yizkor." *Ariel* 13 (1966), p. 39.

Kadmon, Haya. "Never Again!" *Jewish Currents* (January 1961).

Karni, Yehuda. "My Mother." H.H. Fein. *Chapters on Modern Hebrew Literature*. New York: Hadassah, 1947, p. 79.

Katzenelson, Yitzhak. "The Song of the Slaughtered Jewish People." Joseph Leftwich, ed. *The Golden Peacock*. New York: Yoseloff, 1961, pp. 513-516.

Kovner, Abba. *A Canopy in the Desert*. Shirley Kaufman, trans. Pittsburgh: University of Pittsburgh Press, 1972.

Schneor, Zalman. "The Middles Ages are Coming." Ruth Finer Mintz, ed. *Modern Hebrew Poetry*. Berkeley and Los Angeles: University of California Press, 1968, pp. 90-95.

Shimoni, David. "And Should the Wonder Happen." Penueli and Ukhmani, eds. *Anthology of Modern Hebrew Poetry*. Jerusalem: Israel Universities Press.

Shlonsky, Avraham. "Inquire, Your Burned in Fire." Yaacov Shilhav, *Flame and Fury*. Based on the publications of Yad Vashem, ed. Sarah Feinstein. New York: Jewish Education Committee Press, 1962, p. 13.

———. "Oath," op. cit., p. 5.

SECONDARY SOURCES

Alter, Robert. *After the Tradition: Essays on Modern Jewish Writing*. New York: Dutton, 1968.

Bar Natan, Moshe. "Two Novels." *Jewish Frontier* (October, 1965).

Gross, Natan. *Ha-Shoah ba-Shirah ha-Ivrit* (Hebrew). Yad Va-Shem: Kibbutz ha-Meuhad, 1974.

Halkin, Simon. *Modern Hebrew Literature: From the Enlightenment to the Birth of the State of Israel*. New York: Schocken, 1970.

Halperin, Irving. "Spiritual Resistence in Holocaust Literature." *Yad Bashem Studies III*. Jerusalem: Yad Vashem, 1968.

———. "Israel, the Holocaust, and the Survivors." *Reconstructionist* (April 15, 1966).

Kressel, Getzel. *Lexicon ha-Sifrut ha-Ivrit bi-Dorot ha-Aharonim* (Hebrew) 2 vols. Merhavia: Kibbutz ha-Artzl, 1965.

Kurzweil, Baruch. *Ben Hazon u-Ven ha-Absurdi* (Hebrew). Jerusalem: Schocken, 1968.

Malkin, B.D. "The Holocaust Literature as Reflected in the Literature of the Land." *The Institute of Jewish Affairs Anniversary Volume* (1941-1961).

Newman, Aryeh. "Gleanings from Holocaust Literature." *Jewish Heritage* (Summer, 1961).

Robinson, Jacob. *The Holocaust and After: Sources and Literature in English*. Jerusalem: Israel Universities Press, 1973.

Yudkin, Leon I. *Escape into Siege: A Survey of Israeli Literature Today*. London: Routledge and Kegan Paul, 1974.